COUNTER THREAT

My Life Inside the Other Secret Service

By STEVEN M. SCHENCK
Former Special Agent & Agent in Charge
US Department of State
Diplomatic Security Service

Chapbook Press

Schuler Books
2660 28th Street SE
Grand Rapids, MI 49512 (616)
942-7330
www.schulerbooks.com

Counter Threat: My Life Inside the Other Secret Service

ISBN 13: 9781948237765

Library of Congress Control Number: 2021905076

To contact the author: Bondman005@yahoo.com

The opinions, comments, observations, and historical references in this book are from the author's own recollections, notes, and research, and do not necessarily represent the opinions of the Government of the United States, including the State Department or the Bureau of Diplomatic Security. The Public Affairs Office of the US State Department has edited and approved this book (with modifications) for publishing. Over eighty pages had to be revised so as not to expose what the State Department considers to be still classified or sensitive information.

The author is satisfied that the editing has not disturbed the general content and message he wishes to convey.

Printed in the United States by Chapbook Press.

ACKNOWLEDGEMENTS

I wish to acknowledge the brave men and women of the Diplomatic Security Service, the US Foreign Service, and the USMC Marine Security Guards of whom this book is about.

My heartfelt thanks are also extended to my parents, Bob, and Eleanor Schenck, for providing me with a safe and loving home environment, a good education, and for encouraging me to be all that I could be.

CONTENTS

PROLOGUE

This long tradition of diplomacy . . . has been marked by more sacrifice than most Americans will ever know. There are few professions more dangerous than the practice of foreign affairs, and there are few professionals who put more on the line for this nation than the agents of the Diplomatic Security Service.

RICHARD L. ARMITAGE, DEPUTY SECRETARY
AT THE GRADUATION CEREMONY FOR
DS SPECIAL AGENTS, JAN. 29, 2003

Scene: CIA Analyst Jack Ryan (Harrison Ford) is at home entertaining the British Foreign Secretary. Suddenly the house plunges into darkness and gunfire erupts. Ryan frantically searches the premises for help, only to find one of the US Special Agents lying dead on the front porch. Grabbing the fallen agent's two-way radio, Ryan pleads anxiously for help: "This is Ryan . . . any DS agent? Any DS agent? This is Ryan . . . anybody?"

The above scene is from the movie *Patriot Games* (Paramount Pictures, 1992), based on the novel by Tom Clancy. It is one of the few, film references to the DS (Diplomatic Security Service), a little known, partially covert, law-enforcement, security, and counterterrorism bureau within the US State Department.

This book is a compilation of true stories about my life and the dangerous encounters I faced while protecting US ambassadors, Secretary of State Kissinger and Mrs. Kissinger, other diplomats, and Peace Corps volunteers abroad during historic world events. From 1974 to 1981, I served as Special Agent/Chicago Field Office, Senior Resident Agent/Detroit, Special Agent in Charge of Dignitary Protection Details, and as Regional Security Officer overseas protecting US ambassadors and diplomats. My service in these positions has been with the US Department of State's Diplomatic Security Service, also known as Diplomatic Security (abbreviated as DSS or DS). Since 1994, I have been under contract with DS as Special Investigator. I also perform special investigations under contract for other federal agencies and have been an international security consultant for private corporations. Doubtless few have ever heard of DS or its often-covert missions to counter terrorism and enhance national security. Like the Secret Service, Diplomatic Security Special Agents also have the duty of dignitary protection. The Secret Service has the responsibility for protecting the president, vice president, their families, and visiting heads of State such as a president, prime minister, or king of a foreign country. By Congressional authority, DS is charged with the protection of Secretaries of State and their families and all other foreign leaders visiting the United States. When I was appointed to become Special Agent in 1974, the Diplomatic Security Service was expanding from 400 agents to over 800 in response to a wave of terrorist acts abroad. Our embassies were being bombed, and American ambassadors and other diplomats were being kidnapped and killed. Today DS is comprised of over 3000 highly trained men and women. Due in part to the blame for failure that DS suffered because of the Benghazi attack, the organization is increasing the number of personnel again. Missions of the Diplomatic Security Service are dangerous and diverse. DS has a domestic mission within the US and an international mission abroad. Within the US, DS agents are summoned frequently from the various field offices around the country to engage in dignitary protection assignments. Teams are formed to protect foreign dignitaries visiting the US. This includes vice presidents, foreign ministers, or other dignitary notables, some of whom are known to be specific targets for assassination. DS also operates a permanent security team (Detail) 24/7 to protect the Secretary of State and his or her family, their residence, and all their movements. Within the US and abroad, DS agents investigate and bring to justice perpetrators of passport and visa fraud. DS provides cooperation and active assistance to Interpol, the FBI, and the CIA with investigations of international crime, criminals, and terrorists. DS Agents in foreign countries assist the US Secret Service with international visits by the US President. DS Special Investigators conduct personnel security investigations of applicants for national security positions within the US and throughout the world. Special Investigators also perform the required periodic security review investigations of incumbents. Anyone holding a national security clearance must have his or her background reviewed periodically through investigation.

Internationally, the mission of DS is to counter the threat *(Counter Threat)* of kidnappings, crime, terrorism, and espionage. DS protects US ambassadors and US embassy and consulate personnel and manages the security of such facilities. Just as American diplomats carry diplomatic passports, so do DS agents assigned to foreign posts. Yet, DS personnel must also carry guns and act at times with counter-measures to threats while protecting the diplomats on foreign soil. When necessary, such engagements ignore the non-combative, diplomatic role of negotiating conflicts, i.e., the rules of diplomacy. In foreign countries, DS agents are gun-toting, highly-trained civilians operating as diplomats on foreign soil, carefully balancing yet sometimes ignoring the rules of diplomacy while engaged in their mission to protect diplomats and classified information. Teams of specially trained agents are deployed to high-threat locations. DS Regional Security Officers (RSOs) are stationed at every US embassy. They manage the protection of US diplomats, embassies, consulates, and other US government facilities in foreign countries. RSOs are the civilian managers of the US Marine Security Guard detachments at embassies and consulates. RSOs work closely with the Marine Master Gunnery Sergeants who directly supervise the MSGs. The Bureau of Diplomatic Security oversees private security contractors hired by companies such as Blackwater USA (renamed in 2009 to XE Services), Dyncorp, Aegis, Triple Canopy, and others. These brave men and women augment the State Department personnel as they work to assist DS in dangerous, foreign environments including Iraq and Afghanistan.

INTRODUCTION

Counter Threat: My Life Inside the Other Secret Service presents the reader with a first-hand account of my experiences training for and engaged in the mission of protecting US diplomats and embassies in foreign countries, and within the United States. The details of the training and of the missions have never been revealed except for brief newspaper accounts of the dignitaries' visits. Now, after twenty-five years, the stories can be told. You will gain insight as to the character of those dark-suited warriors wearing dark sunglasses who are protecting important dignitaries. The book reveals details of dangerous rides in motorcades while encountering threats with Secretary of State Henry Kissinger in Israel, and diplomats in El Salvador, during a raging civil war. There, I lead teams of Special Agents charged with the protection of two US ambassadors during three years of civil unrest and war. One of the ambassadors, along with the Deputy Chief of Mission, three other agents and I are taken hostage, and the embassy is stormed by an angry mob. I also write of my desperate efforts to save the life of a kidnapped businessman and to rescue an endangered Peace Corps volunteer. *Counter Threat* also exposes new and startling facts about the failed hostage rescue of American diplomats in Teheran, and of a serious breach of security aboard *Air Force One* that imperils everyone, including the Secretary of State. I share my memoirs of guarding the Kissinger's while on Middle East peace missions. Other chapters provide details of guarding the infamous Imelda Marcos, in New York City. Often these missions included first-hand encounters with celebrities such as Elizabeth Taylor, Andy Warhol, and Van Cliburn. I also share a very personal account of my family's attempt to adopt an abandoned infant and of a bomb explosion near the infant's crib.   The identities of those with whom I served, including DS, CIA and military intelligence officers may not have been revealed. Their names may be protected by pseudonyms. What is more, a few of the action accounts are slightly fictionalized. This was done for two reasons: first, to protect the identity of the CIA, DS and Special Ops, military personnel and Marines involved and second, to give the reader a more comprehensive account of how DS agents and Marine Security Guards fight off an attack on an embassy. I have combined the accounts of two separate attacks into one. I hope you will find missions and historic events described in this book to be exciting and revealing. There are chapters in which I recount missions as a Special Agent and Special Agent in Charge protecting dignitaries while they visited the US. The book describes the elaborate planning performed by agents in preparation for official and unofficial visits. Sometimes the unofficial dignitary visits involved protecting their families, for example, while vacationing at Disney World or other destinations. Most visits, however, were for official business to

Washington, D.C., or to New York and the United Nations. I reveal the factual details of the visits, including threats encountered. In a second book currently being written, I reveal very personal accounts of what the DS agents endure and the challenges they face when protecting the foreign dignitaries inside the US.

CHAPTER 1

Benghazi, Libya: The Second 9/11 Attack

On September 11, 2012, another 9/11 terrorist attack occurred against the United States. Four American diplomats, including Ambassador Christopher Stevens, were killed, and several security officers were wounded in an attack on the consulate in Benghazi, Libya. This was an act of war. By way of international law, the land upon which US embassies and consulates are built throughout the world has long been established as "US Soil." Thus, the attack in Benghazi that killed and wounded Americans was carried out on US soil, clearly making this an act of war. As Commander in Chief, President Obama should have acted immediately. But the Obama Administration crafted a cover-up. Secretary of State Hillary Clinton, US Ambassador to the United Nations Christina Rice and other officials at the White House conspired in perpetrating the cover-up.

The cover-up began when UN Ambassador Rice (President Obama's appointed envoy) appeared on several television news shows two days after the incident, proclaiming the attack as an act of rebellion by Muslims. She claimed that Muslims in Egypt, Libya, and elsewhere were protesting to show their outrage at an anti-Islam YouTube video made by a private party in the United

States. This song and dance were perpetrated for three weeks by the president, Clinton, as well as White House Press Secretary Jay Carney and Ambassador Rice. The White House and Secretary of State Clinton made numerous denials regarding previous communications sent by security officers and Ambassador Stevens from Tripoli requesting security enhancements. Lieutenant Colonel Andrew Wood was in command of a team of US military special-operations personnel known as the Security Support Team (SST). He and his team were charged with providing additional security support to US personnel stationed in Libya. I also used special operations personnel during missions to protect US ambassadors. They were there at the behest of the State Department to provide additional protection. Wood testified that he sent cables repeatedly requesting that the SST be extended to also support the consulate in Benghazi. He testified before Congressional committees investigating the Benghazi tragedy that his requests were denied. Eric Nordstrom—former Chief Security Officer (Regional Security Officer) for DS in Tripoli—testified that he repeatedly sent memos to DS Headquarters in March and July of 2012, requesting security upgrades and additional Special Agents for Ambassador Steven's protection. Neither of the requests, however, received any response. Deputy Assistant Secretary for Security Charlene Lamb testified that these requests were taken to be suggestions rather than requests for assistance, a statement vehemently denied by RSO Nordstrom.

Adding to the cover-up was a deliberate redaction of the word "terrorism" or "terrorists" from a CIA classified memo to the White House regarding the Benghazi attack. The media speculated that the reasons for the cover-up were to divert negative attention from President Obama during the approaching re-election campaign. But a persistent press and Congress insisted on getting answers. Were President Obama and Secretary Clinton at fault for not heeding Ambassador Stevens' requests for more security, and, if so, responsible for the deaths of four brave American diplomats? While Americans were dying in Benghazi, bureaucrats in Washington were debating as to whether to send a US military combat force dressed in uniform or in civilian clothing. Ultimately, no one was officially sent. A self-imposed team of US Defense contractors left Tripoli and went to Benghazi but were too late to save the Ambassador. Two of the contractors were killed in that team's efforts to rescue Ambassador Stevens and Sean Smith, a US Foreign Service officer.

As my book will describe in greater detail, I was a Regional Security Officer II (RSO) engaged in countering terrorist attacks and protecting US ambassadors. A US ambassador is personally appointed by the president of the United States to serve as his personal envoy in a foreign country. When the ambassador writes and sends classified cable messages to Washington, D.C., the White House and the Secretary of State are direct recipients. This was true of "Action Required" cables sent by ambassadors during my watch as an RSO II at US Embassy San Salvador, El Salvador (1979-1981), during a raging civil war. The protocol remains the same today. Classified cables, especially those regarding needs for enhanced security due to threats, demonstrations and terrorist actions are directed to the White House and to the Secretary of State's team. Any embassy or consulate to come under attack would generate a cable to the White House, the State Department, and the CIA. Both President Obama and Secretary of State Clinton had to have known within hours of the attack.

Why and how the attack at Benghazi happened has now (in 2016) been revealed as a deliberate and planned act of terrorism by an Islamic extremist group operating in Libya. Secretary of State Hillary Clinton ultimately stated that she took full responsibility because the attack happened on her watch. She also has since resigned her cabinet post shortly after President Obama began his second term in office. But this was likely her plan and not done consequently, to the 9/11 attack in Benghazi.

On December 3, 2012, I read an unclassified e-mail sent to all State Department personnel that a new position had been created inside DS. This position is entitled "Deputy Assistant Secretary for High Threat Posts (DAS-HT)." Richard M. Wade received the first appointment as the new DAS-HT. The creation of this position stripped Deputy Assistant Secretary for Security Charlene Lamb of some of her responsibilities. On December 19, 2012, three State Department officials resigned under pressure, citing management failures. President Obama and Secretary of State Clinton or their handlers saw to it that others took the fall. They included the Assistant Secretary for Diplomatic Security, Eric J Boswell; Deputy Assistant Secretary Charlene Lamb; and, Raymond Maxwell, the Deputy Assistant Secretary of State who oversaw Libya.

On September 11, 2012—the day of the attack—President Obama was campaigning heavily in his attempt to achieve a second four-year term as President. He was opposed by Republican presidential nominee Mitt Romney. The polls showed the two neck-and-neck as voting day approached. News reports indicated that the president had been absent from the daily White House security briefings at least two times in the two weeks leading up to the attack in Benghazi. On that day he was campaigning in Las Vegas. Upon being told of the attack, he suspended his campaigning and traveled back to D.C. But he took no immediate action to provide additional security and began denying that the attack was a terrorist act or act of war.

After the attack, both the White House and the press reported that not since 1979 has an American ambassador been killed while serving in a foreign post. That incident was the assassination of US Ambassador Adolf "Spike" Dubs in Afghanistan on February 14, 1979. I was serving as the RSO at the US Embassy in El Salvador on the day of that attack. We were on high alert after receiving intelligence reports that other US ambassadors were also being targeted. In my book I provide details of many terrorist incidents which have occurred against US diplomats. The singular, notable US force that protects foreign dignitaries, US diplomats, and counteracts terrorist attacks from raining down on US embassies, consulates, and diplomats throughout the world is the Diplomatic Security Service. The following chapters recount stories about the dignitaries I have protected, and about the danger and anguish I experienced while a Special Agent inside the "other secret service."

CHAPTER 2

THE BOND

Why, you might ask, would anyone go to work each day willing to deliberately step into harm's way and take a bullet or a blade to save someone else? Is it due to training, which attempts to instill into the brain an instantaneous response to throw their body in front of the intended victim, to absorb the threat? Is it an odd, fatalistic superhero syndrome that somehow causes the bodyguard to think he is immortal? Is it so spontaneous, due to the training, that there is not even a second's thought about it? I think it is more than that. I know from being there, from being someone who has thrown my body on top of the intended target of killers, that it is more. Those of us who put our lives at risk protecting dignitaries do not think we are immortal; we are most certainly aware of the prospect that death could become us for our actions. I do not think of myself as a hero, and I don't perform my duties as such. I knew that, if necessary, my life might be sacrificed in the line of duty. True, the training is designed to cause me to act instantaneously, if necessary. But that action is voluntary. Thus, a great deal more than blind heroism is involved.

First, it is a bond that I formed with the protectee that engenders a ready willingness to take that fatal blow. I realize, as I live and breathe with these leaders each day, what special people they are. As such, a bond is formed—an almost inexplicable bond between me as the bodyguard and the dignitary. When Presidents Ford, Reagan and Trump were each shot at, agents immediately and instinctively sheltered them with their own bodies. Those agents, part of the Secret Service Presidential Detail, spent many hours with these two presidents every day. When performing long-term assignments with protectees, we usually come to admire them on a very personal level, which helps to build the bond. Whenever there have been news reports of an assassination or an attempted assassination of a political or world leader in which their bodyguards were killed, I believe those guardians sacrificed their lives out of total commitment to and respect for the dignitaries they were protecting.

Second, like many of my colleagues, I truly admired the commitment and sheer guts exhibited by the world leaders themselves. I often think of the numerous times a protectee has been forewarned by Intelligence sources that an attack may be imminent. Reports may indicate that an attack could come while the dignitary is riding in a motorcade or while giving a speech. Yet, many of these brave leaders forge onward without hesitating. I think of former Secretary of State Henry Kissinger, whom I guarded in the US and throughout the world, often the most wanted target of insurgents in foreign countries. His dedication and belief in furthering efforts for peace in the Middle

East outweighed his concerns for personal safety. How many of us would get into our vehicle and ride to work if someone had said, "a sniper may shoot at your vehicle today" or "we have information that leads us to believe extremists are going to fire a rocket at your vehicle today" or "roadside bombs may have been planted along various routes to be remotely detonated when your car passes by"? Most of us would probably huddle in our homes, locked, and secured. Kissinger and others of the world's diplomats were aware of such reports. Yet, rarely did he allow the threats to dissuade him from carrying out his duties. As one who was charged with protecting him, I admired him greatly for such courage, in the same way other leaders' bodyguards admire those whom they protect.

Thirdly, if the bond between me as an agent and the protectee would not of itself move me to give of my life, then the bond I have to the cause would. I once guarded Yasser Arafat, the famed leader of the Palestinian Liberation Organization (PLO). I have also guarded foreign ministers of Syria, Somalia, and Libya, each of whom was, at one time, considered to be a potential enemy of the US. Whether the dignitaries come from countries that are close allies of the United States or from those that are political opponents or adversaries, these are great people nonetheless. They are world leaders. They may be Communists, Middle Eastern extremists, or supporters of terrorism. Yet, they have risen to the highest political status--that of Head of State or another high-ranking official. These leaders are revered by their fellow countrymen and people of their region. Each Special Agent knows that, should a ranking dignitary of a foreign nation be injured or killed while visiting the US, his fellow countrymen would die in part, too. Such a catastrophe may cause that leader's nation to suspect the US of intentional neglect. Diplomatic relations between that leader's country and the US could suffer a tremendous setback. In countries where relationships with the US are tenuous or hostile, negative propaganda against the United States would likely be generated. Peoples in such nations would believe or be led to believe that US Special Agents did not try hard enough to protect their leader. Adversaries might conjure up a conspiracy theory, suggesting that the US was behind the assassination or attempt. Those of us whose job it is to protect such dignitaries realize all these possibilities and would therefore make that ultimate sacrifice for the good of our nation.

Finally, a bond also forms because these leaders are human beings, with personal hearts and souls that are as passionate as each of us perceive our own to be. With few exceptions, they do what they think is best for their people and their nation. They trust that DS and Secret Service agents will protect their lives when they are visiting in the US. That trust is the essence of our ability to protect the dignitary. Without their trust and cooperation, our mission would fail. So, those of us dedicated to performing the mission of protecting foreign dignitaries on our soil take trust as the absolute determiner of performance. This will only come about through repeated successful performances, which eventually gain us a reputation for being completely dedicated and professionally competent.

Agents who protect dignitaries have no political opinion or preference regarding the protectee. Each dignitary is treated with equal professionalism and respect. Those who rely on us for their safety have studied how US Special Agents have performed in the line of duty. They are aware of the rigorous physical and mental training we have undergone. They know of the success we have had in preventing assassination attempts against foreign and US leaders. There have been assassination attempts of foreign leaders while visiting the US. In each attempt the expertise of DS or Secret Service agents has prevailed, and the leader has been spared harm. Foreign leaders would insist on their own bodyguards to protect them if they did not trust that we would protect them at all costs.

CHAPTER 3

A PROVIDENTIAL ENCOUNTER

I grew up in the town of Granville, Michigan, graduating from Grandville High School in 1965. Grandville is in Kent County, a suburb of Grand Rapids. Inspired by a grandfather who was a respected Detective Lieutenant with the Kent County Sheriff's Department and by James Bond films, I was self-driven to acquire a career in law enforcement preferably federal or international in scope. By end of high school my vocational direction was clear. I was determined to do whatever it took to become a federal agent or an Intelligence officer with any of the following agencies: Central Intelligence Agency (CIA), National Security Agency (NSA), Federal Bureau of Investigation (FBI), Secret Service, Drug Enforcement Administration (DEA), Alcohol, Tobacco Tax and Firearms (ATF), US Customs Enforcement, US Postal Inspectors' Service. Knowing that to be successful in my pursuit, I would require the completion of a four-year degree, I enrolled in a social science, undergraduate program with emphasis in Criminal Justice at near-by Grand Valley State University. I also visited the local offices of agencies in Grand Rapids to make appointments and speak to real-life Special Agents. The FBI, the Secret Service, US Postal Inspectors' Service, and others were very accommodating to young inquirers. I learned that to successfully qualify for the position of an FBI Special Agent an applicant needed a graduate level degree in law, accounting, foreign language, or the physical sciences. All the agencies preferred an applicant with an undergraduate degree and several years of what the agencies termed as "relevant leadership experience." These consisted of the basic pre-requisite qualifications in the 1960s. Since then, these requirements have changed somewhat to include high-tech skills in many different areas, especially information technology, forensic and computer sciences. Four years later, in 1969, I graduated from Grand Valley with a BA in Sociology and a minor in Psychology. I knew I did not want to continue with more academic work. I was anxious to fulfill the prerequisite of several years of relevant leadership experience. So, I began seeking jobs I thought would fill the bill. At twenty-one, I answered an ad in the local paper for a parttime, reserve police officer position in the nearby town of Hudsonville, Michigan. I was hired. Hudsonville remains, a small and quiet community of about five thousand residents with twenty churches. The town had a very conservative, predominantly Dutch Protestant, Reformed, and Christian Reformed populace. For many years, there were no permitted alcohol sales, or taverns. There was little trouble in the town, except for the occasional traffic crash, a break-in here and there, or the odd noise complaint. However, a busy four-lane highway ran right through the center of town, serving as the major artery connecting Grand Rapids with Lake Michigan and the metropolitan areas of Gary, Indiana and Chicago, Illinois. The Chief of Police often cautioned his reserve officers about all the undesirable characters and contraband that traversed the highway then, and that continues to do so to this day. He often warned me to be very careful during traffic stops. The police chief was Hudsonville's only full-time cop. The reserve force of six part-time officers, now including me, filled in on nights, weekends, and holidays. Clad in full officer's uniform, strapping a Sam Brown gun belt complete with a .357 Magnum, mace, handcuffs, badge, and cap, I took the wheel of the patrol car. For three months, senior reserve officers trained me. After a total of six months as a part-time reserve officer and with the completion of college, Hudsonville hired me full-time. I attended twelve weeks at a Michigan Law Enforcement Officers' Training Academy in Lansing, returning to begin a career as a full-fledged police officer. A year later, I accepted a better paying position as a road deputy, with the Ottawa County Sheriff's Department. To become a uniformed cop working in a police cruiser would have been many a young person's dream that came true. For me, it only meant a stepping stone to bigger things. My sights continued to be set much higher--that of becoming a federal agent or spy.

By now it was 1972. Watergate, that infamous debacle that eventually brought President Nixon to a disgraceful end, was emerging onto the political scene. The Vietnam War was raging, with the result that the United States was never more divided in all its history, save during the Civil War. Illegal drug use on college campuses was rampant, even spreading into middle schools and high schools. I was working in my third year as a uniformed patrol officer. While I searched vehicles and persons for small amounts of illegal drugs, the federal army of the DEA was making huge busts and, in conjunction with the CIA, FBI, Secret Service, and ATF, making all the headlines. Reading these headlines making news stories repeatedly reminded me of the goal I so sorely sought, namely a job as a federal agent. Every month, I had sent out several letters of inquiry, along with the standard federal application forms to a long list of agencies. Nevertheless, the applications were always returned with the words "Not Hiring" or "Thank you for your application."

I decided to go after more "leadership experience." I left uniformed police work and became a security manager for Meijer Incorporated, a retail department and grocery megastore, where I gained another eighteen months of on-the-job experience, managing a security department of 30 employees.

While working to gain the "relevant" experience, I wrote a letter to my congressman, to inquire as to anything he could do to help me land a job as a federal agent. The distinguished Gerald R. Ford was Congressman for the Fifth District, State of Michigan, representing Grand Rapids and Kent County in

Washington, D.C. Congressman Ford had a habit of coming to his district to talk to his constituents. He often used a 1972 Winnebago motor home as a mobile office, taking it to different parts of town on his visits. Much to my surprise, Ford responded by informing me that he would soon be visiting Grand Rapids and offering me a personal appointment. And so it was that one summer day in 1972 I sat down with Congressman Jerry Ford, as he liked to be known, in a one-on-one meeting in his motor home. The Winnebago was parked in a city parking lot in Grandville, with only one other person--his Administrative Assistant--in attendance. We talked for about thirty minutes. First, I told him of my fervent career aspirations and described what I had done to prepare for them. He seemed to take a liking to me, saying he had a son about my age, also named Steve. He said that he would like to help me with my career, but that there was a general hiring freeze with most of the agencies to which I had been making applications and that he expected the freeze to last for another year or two. He explained that the Vietnam War was costing the US government a lot of money. Consequently, funding for other needs was scarce. I felt the sinking feeling of rejection. But then Congressman Ford enlightened and uplifted me with fresh information. He told me that he sat on the House Appropriations Committee, which oversees funding for the US State Department. He added that the problems of terrorism, terrorist threats, and threats of assassination against our diplomatic personnel and missions abroad and against foreign dignitaries visiting the US were growing concerns. As a result, the expansion of a little-known security/counterintelligence agency within the State Department was underway. This agency, the Office of Security, later to be renamed the Diplomatic Security Service, was being formed as a discreet protection and counterterrorism service. It was designed to be small-- comprising about eight hundred people who were to be highly trained by State Department Instructors, the Secret Service, FBI, CIA, and the US Navy Explosive Ordinance Command (EOD), in matters of dignitary protection, perimeter and building security, investigation, and counter terrorism. These men and women would be subject to assignments and duties worldwide. Congressman Ford went on to say that many of the details about the new agency were still classified but added that if I did want to apply, I should send him my résumé, which he would forward to the appropriate people at the State Department. With a grateful "Thank you" and a handshake, I departed the motor home. 'Oh My God,' I said to myself, as the adrenalin rushed through my body and brain! This was beyond my wildest expectations: here was a multi-tasked agency that combined all the services each of the others performed singularly! Countless nights of prayers had been answered! Hope sprang eternal, as the saying goes.

I went directly home that same afternoon and cranked out a fresh résumé and a cover letter on the typewriter, for

Congressman Ford, referring to the interview with him and again expressing my sincere gratitude. I then rushed off to the post office with the letter, paid for the fastest mail delivery possible and sent it off. I think the polished résumé arrived at Congressman Ford's desk in Washington probably even before he had returned from his visit to Michigan. He had forewarned me that any efforts he made on my behalf in no way meant an automatic appointment. Even if I got a call, he said, I still would have to pass a series of rigorous interviews and a thorough background investigation. He also cautioned me that these things took time and not to expect anything too soon. He concluded that he was only facilitating the process so that my résumé got to the right place. Months passed by. I continued working as Security Manager with Meijer. Finally, I got the call in the fall of 1973, some fifteen months later. I was instructed to go to the Chicago Field Office of the Office of Security for the US State Department, located in the Everett Dirksen Building, the location of the interviews. The interviews were intense. The Special Agents that conducted the interviews wanted to know every detail of my life from age eighteen forward. I was asked to opine on many subjects, including the Vietnam War, the use of marijuana and other forms of drugs and hallucinogens, the criminal justice system, foreign affairs current at that time. In addition, I was asked about my personal likes and dislikes, including having to answer numerous questions relative to my family background, growing up, and how I went about selecting my friends. Following the interviews, I waited anxiously while an intense background investigation was being completed. A Special Agent from the Office of Security was combing the greater Grand Rapids area, Grandville, Hudsonville, and Ottawa County, interviewing sources, and reviewing records of places I had lived, worked, or attended school since the age of seventeen. Yet no notification of hiring came for me during the remainder of that year.

But one morning in mid-January 1974 the phone rang just as I was about to leave my house and go to work. I answered, and a voice with a distinct, southern accent, said,

"Hello, Steven, this is John Richardson, Special Agent in Charge of the Chicago Field Office of State Department Security calling . . . how are you today?"

"Just fine, sir . . . and yourself?" My heart immediately began beating faster, perspiration starting to build on my hands!

"Fine . . . fine. I am calling this morning to offer you a position as Special Agent with us. If you accept, you would need to report to the Chicago Field Office within two weeks. I know it is rather short notice, but we have several others joining also, and we need to start a training session." Richardson went on to describe the starting pay and government benefit package I would be receiving. But I barely paid attention. Instead, my mind whirled into a highspeed rewind of everything I had thought of, dreamed of, prayed for, and worked for since high school, in the hopes of receiving this very phone call! All those years of going after my goal had paid off. A question from Richardson brought me back to the present moment.

"Would you like some time to think this over, talk it over with your wife perhaps?"

"Sir, my wife, and I have already done so in hopes that this call would come one day. I accept the offer with gratitude. Just tell me where to report and when." Richardson chuckled and finished telling me the details. He congratulated me on receiving the appointment, and in return I heartily thanked him. With that the call ended. Two weeks later, I reported for duty to the Chicago Field Office, as Special Agent Steven Schenck, US State Department, Diplomatic Security.

As I look back to that meeting with then Congressman Ford, the most astonishing thing of all--unbeknownst at the time to either the Congressman or me--was that in 1975, less than two years later, we would meet again. In those subsequent meetings, however, I would be escorting foreign dignitaries under my protection into the Oval Office of the White House. These foreign leaders had scheduled appointments as I once did, only now with President Gerald R. Ford!

As it went, by 1973 Gerald Ford had served as United States Congressman representing the Fifth District of Michigan, my home district, for twenty-five years. He was also the Minority

Leader in the House of Representatives from 1965 to 1973. In the fall of 1973, the Watergate scandal was brewing under the presidency of Richard M. Nixon, with political casualties on the rise. Vice President Spiro T. Agnew had been found to be involved in illegal financial proceedings and soon resigned in disgrace. President Nixon appointed Gerald Ford to be the new vice president. Three months later, I received notification of my official appointment to that of Special Agent.

I sent a letter to Vice President Ford, informing him of my appointment and thanking him for his guidance. I also congratulated him on becoming VP. Ever kind and responsive to his constituents, he likewise sent a letter back to me, personally signed on stationery captioned *The Vice President, Washington* in the upper right margin, and with the logo of the Great Seal in the upper left margin, congratulating me upon my appointment to Special Agent.

On December 27, 2006 President Ford passed away at the age of ninety-three. He died peacefully at home, his wife, and children by his bedside. I hope President Ford is remembered by the country for how great a president he was. Though he was never elected to the office of vice president or president, I think he was 'elected' by the Almighty to assume the leading role to see the American people through one of the darkest periods in our nation's history --"A Time to Heal," was a phrase used by President Ford, during that time. It became the title of a book later written by him. Of all the Presidents, he will be remembered as one of the most decent and honest, just the man that was needed to move our country forward after Watergate. The meeting I personally had with then Congressman Ford in his modest, motor home office back in 1972 shall ever be remembered as a providential encounter.

CHAPTER 4
AN EVENING TO REMEMBER

One afternoon in October 1977, I was in Chicago to attend a Field Office Conference. I was now serving as Senior Resident Agent for Diplomatic Security, in Detroit, since June of 1975. I returned to the Chicago Field Office four times annually for a general meeting and firearms qualification. My duties as a Senior Resident Agent included being an Agent in Charge (AIC) of protective security Details, for foreign dignitaries visiting the US. It was 3:30 p.m. The other Chicago based agents and I had returned from the firing range. We were busy cleaning our weapons when I heard my name being summoned over the intercom by John Richardson the Special Agent in Charge (SAIC) of the Chicago Field Office. "Will Steve Schenck please come to my office?"   As I entered his office he said to me, "Mrs. Marcos is coming to the US again, Steve, and she has specifically requested you to be the AIC of her protective security detail. Are you up for it?" John chuckled, knowing of the First Lady's reputation amongst DS for keeping agents up very late, working long hours. "Why not?" I replied with a grin. "There's never a dull moment when she's around!"

"Better you than me," John quipped. I had first protected First Lady Marcos, in the spring of 1977, when she came to New York for an unofficial visit.

I knew of John's sentiments. John Richardson had just entered his thirtieth year of civil service, twenty of which had been with DS. He was in his mid-fifties and was a brilliant administrator. John's easy going southern manner (born and raised in Georgia) and encouraging, yet methodical approach to leadership made him one of the best SAICs the DS has ever had. Each new agent that was assigned to the Chicago Field Office, and many who were there as experienced agents, had learned to become better skilled through John's leadership. But John did not particularly like dignitary protection work. He was an excellent investigator, expertly skilled in conducting personnel security investigations, (national security background investigations). This was his forte. John continued speaking.

"Apparently, Mrs. Marcos made this request through her emissary in Washington, who, in turn, informed Mr. Dikeos at the State Department, who then called me. Dikeos told me that Mrs. Marcos had been impressed by the job you did as AIC in April when she came to New York."

Richardson, who was standing arm's length from me in his office, laid his hand on my right shoulder and said, "Steve, I would consider this an honor if I were you--that a notable dignitary such as Mrs. Marcos had specifically requested you. The Director was very pleased, and so am I. Keep up the good work"

"Thanks, John" I replied. "I will do my best. When will she be arriving?"

"In a few weeks . . . sometime in early to mid-November for the UNGA" (United Nations General Assembly.)

Prior to working my first Marcos detail earlier that year, I had been fully briefed about the assassination attempt on Mrs. Marcos' life. Mrs. Marcos held the dubious distinction of being amongst a select few world leaders to have experienced an assassination attempt on their lives. She had been seriously wounded. The frightful event was forever etched in her mind. No doubt that she was constantly anxious about her personal safety. Knowing of this history, the agents and I were even more alert and prepared. We were very aware that each time she visited the US she was putting her trust and confidence in the other Special Agents and me--that we would keep her safe from harm. She was putting her life in our hands.

The attack had come on December 7, 1972, while Mrs. Marcos was the guest of honor at a National Beautification and Cleanliness contest in Manila. As the ceremony was being broadcast on live TV, one of the award recipients wearing a long, graduation style robe suddenly left the lineup and thrust toward Mrs. Marcos. His concealed arms and hands emerged from his robe brandishing a razor sharp, 21" Katipunan bolo knife, and lunged at her. Mrs. Marcos instinctively threw up her arms and hands to block the assault. Blood spurted everywhere as the assassin slashed at her with his blade, carving flesh wounds on her hands, neck, and upper chest! A Philippine congressman and a program official grappled with the assassin. Finally, armed security guards who had been standing well away from Marcos began firing. The assassin, Carlito Dimahilig, was shot from behind. He died on the spot with two bullets in his back. The First Lady had reacted quickly and instinctively by stepping backward when attacked from the front. Luckily, the wounds were not deep. Still, it took over seventy stitches to sew up slash wounds received in the attack. The motive for the attack could have been in response to the president--Ferdinand Marcos--who had suspended the constitution and declared martial law less than three months earlier. Much is made of the fact that the usual security forces had been deliberately moved away from the stage area. Examination of the film, which was broadcast time and again on Philippines television over the next several days, showed the assassin appear to look over his shoulder before attacking as though waiting for a signal, but the glance was not conducive to conclusive evaluation.

October 1977 vanished quickly into November, and with it the commencement of my second Marcos security detail. Marcos had arrived in New York to be the official delegate on behalf of the Philippines to the UN General Assembly.

One evening during her ten-day visit, she and acclaimed concert pianist, Van Cliburn, attended a performance of the world-famous Bolshoi Opera, direct from Moscow. In the 1970s Mrs. Marcos was rumored to be one of the wealthiest women in the world. Van Cliburn was at that time world-renowned. He had thrilled millions of people with his unmatched performances. He had asked Mrs. Marcos to join him for the evening's performance. The two were close, personal friends. Mrs. Marcos met Van Cliburn in 1973 at a special clinic for the care and treatment of hands. Her hands had been severely lacerated during the assassination attempt. Cliburn routinely visited the clinic to receive examinations and special treatments for the tools of his trade--those magnificent hands. Cliburn had previously been invited to perform in the Philippines and to play at the Presidential Palace several times thereafter by President and Mrs. Marcos.

Cliburn was born in Louisiana, July 7, 1934. At age six, he and his parents moved to Texas. By age twelve the child prodigy had won every major local piano competition. At age twenty, Cliburn thrilled the music world with his performance of Tchaikovsky's *Piano Concerto No. 1* during his debut at Carnegie Hall. The concerto was to become his signature piece in performances thereafter. Perhaps his most important and greatest performance was given at the First Tchaikovsky International Piano Competition held in Moscow in 1958. Van was twenty-four years old. The Cold War between the Soviet Union and the Western world was heating up, and Russian Premier Nikita Khrushchev was in attendance. Of the dozen competitors only a Russian concert pianist, Lev Vlasenko, was any real challenger. But in the end, the Russian pianist proved no match for Cliburn's brilliant performance. Still, several of the Soviet judges, anticipating Khrushchev's likely indignation, voted for the Russian competitor. The non-Russian judges sensed what was happening, giving Cliburn perfect scores of 25 on a scale of 0 to 25. Van Cliburn easily won the competition. More important to world history, he won the heart of the Russian Premier, who embraced Cliburn's performance and physically embraced the winner after the competition much to the embarrassment of the Russian judges. *TIME Magazine* put him on their cover, proclaiming him "The Texan Who Conquered Russia." RCA signed him to an exclusive contract, and his recording of Tchaikovsky's *Piano Concerto No. 1* became the first classical album to sell a million copies. It was the best-selling classical album in the world for more than a decade, eventually going triple platinum.

Mrs. Marcos, Van Cliburn, and I were seated together in the eighth Row, main floor of the Metropolitan Opera House. Briefly during the evening's performance, part of me was contemplating in awe of where I was and whose company I was keeping. Just four years earlier I had been living in Grandville, Michigan, working as a security manager and dreaming of one day becoming a federal agent who would be engulfed in assignments of international intrigue. Now that dream had become a reality. There I was: sitting with Van Cliburn, the celebrated classical pianist and Imelda Marcos, the famed and controversial political figure, the First Lady of the president of the Philippines. Though I was in the close company of these two extraordinary people, my mind was still fixed on my duties--guarding the First Lady and managing the detail of DS Special Agents assigned to do the same. The Agent in Charge is the decision-maker for all the security measures required to protect a visiting dignitary, and ultimately responsible for the supervision of the other agents of the detail comprised this time of twelve Special Agents, including one female agent. As AIC, I was prepared, in the event of any kind of an attack upon Mrs. Marcos, to use my body as a shield in a final effort to prevent a bullet or blade from meeting the assassin's mark.

CHAPTER 5

MENACE AT THE MET

Van Cliburn sat next to Mrs. Marcos, on her left, facing the stage. I was sitting in the only other available seat, which was to the left of Van Cliburn. Though not officially under our protection, I believe the other agents and I would have laid down our lives for Van, just as we would have for Mrs. Marcos. The gifted and distinguished pianist has often been hailed as having done more for contributing to détente between the former Soviet Union and the United States than any diplomat or world leader.

Despite his renowned and artistic virtuosity, he was one of the most down to earth, gracious, and compassionate persons I had ever met. The Bolshoi is performed entirely in the Russian language. Realizing that I did not speak Russian and that I had little experience with opera, he was kind enough to interpret various scenes for me. Of course, my job wasn't to enjoy the opera. Yet, part of my training had included behaving diplomatically when spoken to by the dignitaries or their associates. I accepted Van's explanation in a gracious manner. All the while a blanket of agents was covering the exits, lobbies, and vehicles that comprised the waiting motorcade. My radio earpiece crackled with the dialogue of DS agents as they intermittently communicated with the Shift Leader. The Shift Leader supervised the other agents during the event so that I didn't have to give commands while in proximity of the protectee. One of his duties was to walk from post to post, checking on each agent's well-being or to relieve an agent so he or she could have a break.

Mrs. Marcos enjoyed the opera immensely. She told me that she was in such a great mood that she wanted to continue partying and that she would be going to Sardi's for a late-night dinner and after that for dancing at the 21 Club. Sardi's is one of New York's most prestigious supper clubs. There, one is almost sure to see celebrities on any night. The 21 Club has been one of New York's premier nightspots for decades. Despite block-long lines of people hoping to get inside the club on a Saturday night, there was always immediate seating available for Mrs. Marcos and her guests. Undoubtedly, financial arrangements had been previously made so that she was accommodated whenever she desired to go there.

Using my sleeve microphone, I called by radio to the Senior Shift Leader, Billy Settler.

"Settler . . . this is Schenck. See me right away." Billy came over to where the dignitaries and I were seated in the eighth row of the main floor, whereupon I told him of Mrs. Marcos' wishes. He knew, as we all did, what to do next. While Settler went to prepare for what looked to be a long and complicated night of protective activity, Mrs. Marcos, Van Cliburn, and I viewed the second half of the performance. The fate of the First Lady's safety and whether her Saturday night experience in Manhattan following the opera would be enjoyable or tragic was in the hands of my DS team.

Impromptu decisions made by dignitaries to visit public places or step outside the planned itinerary always got an agent's adrenaline pumping. Much had to be done in so little time and with as much secrecy as possible. Settler radioed to all the agents to remain at their posts and to stand by for new information. Next, he went outside to where the motorcade was parked. He gathered up the drivers and the accompanying police officers. Together they planned the routes we would take to Sardi's and the 21 Club. The Shift Leader ordered the advance agent, who had preceded all of us to the Met, to drive the newly planned route and report back if there were any obstructions or detours. He was to do this as he proceeded to Sardi's to inform the restaurant's senior manager that we would be arriving and thus for him to arrange for seating. The same had to be done at the 21 Club. Managers at elite establishments were accustomed to spur-of-the-moment appearances of dignitaries and celebrities. So, they usually kept a few preferred tables in reserve. The advance agent would be tactful, yet commanding, to arrange for the most secure seating. Restaurant and club owners in New York City and elsewhere understand the tragedy that could result from leaked information about the pending arrival of a dignitary. No one wanted their restaurant to be the place where history might recount an assassination or hostile attack upon a world leader. Consequently, the owners and their managers completely cooperated with us.

With advance arrangement in motion, Settler returned inside the opera house and made a radio announcement to the agents on post. "Attention all agents . . . this is Settler. Immediately following the performance we'll be going to dinner and then to a nightclub." He was careful not to mention locations in case someone might overhear his remarks. DS agents are accustomed to working long hours when engaged in dignitary protection missions. Unlike Secret Service, we were fewer in number and didn't have the luxury of being relieved after an eight-hour shift.

As the opera moved through its acts following the intermission, an incident occurred that caused high anxiety for my team. The evening's manager of the Metropolitan Opera House informed the Shift Leader, who relayed by radio to me, that two patrons in the second balcony had come to him to complain about a man who was seated near them. The man was sitting in a seat that had been vacant during the first half of the performance. The patrons, who had observed Mrs. Marcos and Van Cliburn as we escorted them to their seats prior to the start of the performance, said that they believed the man to be of Middle Eastern descent. He was wearing a long black overcoat and tennis shoes. They further described the man as acting very fidgety and leaning forward as if he were looking in the direction where we were seated. They said that the man was looking all around but not paying attention to the performance. Upon hearing this, I turned to Van Cliburn and politely excused myself for a moment, then got up and stepped to the side aisle to duck into the exit area. Speaking into my sleeve microphone, I softly commanded the Shift Leader, Billy Settler. "Settler . . . this is Schenck. Take the NYPD officer and accompany the manager to check on this guy. See if he has a ticket." "Roger that," Settler replied.

Only the opera house manager had the authority to tell a patron to leave the premises or to request the police to do so. Federal agents did not have the authority to act on a simple trespass violation. NYPD could only remove the person if the manager agreed to sign a complaint. Otherwise, our arrest powers were limited to having probable cause that the man was posing a threat to Mrs. Marcos. I returned to my seat and waited anxiously. I debated whether to ask Van to switch seats with me so I could be closer to Mrs. Marcos, but I decided not to do so since I did not want to inform them of my concern and consequently worry her unnecessarily. Minutes later I turned to look upward to see the man being led out of the upper balcony area. Agent Settler and the plainclothes officer were so close to him he could not have raised his arms without being subdued, though no body search had yet been performed. My earpiece sounded again.

"Schenck . . . Settler. We've got him in the outside hallway. He couldn't produce a ticket, so the opera manager told NYPD he would sign a trespassing complaint. NYPD searched him, but he was unarmed. He has no identification or money." The man was taken out of the opera house to an awaiting police car. Another few minutes and Settler spoke again.

"All clear."

As Settler's words crackled through my earpiece, I breathed a sigh of relief while the First Lady continued enjoying the opera and seemingly unaware of what had just transpired. But I wondered, *Was the vagrant part of a greater conspiracy? Was he a ploy to throw us off guard? Were there others outside the Met who were planning an elaborate attack?* In this business one never knew for sure. We had to always be ready for anything. Settler and another agent headed outside to scout the perimeter of the opera house for any suspicious activity. Seeing none, they returned to help escort Mrs. Marcos out to the awaiting motorcade. There were a standing ovation and several encore bows at the end of the opera. As was pre-planned, Mrs. Marcos, Van Cliburn and I resumed our seats after the performance concluded. Agents moved in from side theater exits and stood around us while the audience began to disperse. Several patrons who had been sitting closest to us recognized Cliburn and Mrs. Marcos. They offered words of greeting and some extended handshakes, which the celebrities graciously acknowledged. Upon my cue, we got up and exited out of the theater, down one flight of stairs and out a side exit door. Mrs. Marcos preferred this method of exit to that of going through the slow moving, jostling crowds bearing down on the main entrance.

The distance from the exit door to the limo was fifty feet. Agents assumed a Diamond Formation around us, with one agent leading, or at point, one agent to each side, and another agent following behind. Anxiously, we escorted them to the waiting limousine. The right rear door of the limo was open. Mrs. Marcos slid in, still unaware of what had transpired or of our concerns that a greater threat may be lurking somewhere nearby. Van Cliburn, all too familiar with the practice of protectees being seated in the right rear passenger's seat of an awaiting limousine, walked around the back of the limo and entered through the left rear door, street side. I entered the right front seat. Once inside, the driver quickly locked the limo doors with the push of a button. The team had the limousine surrounded. Then I waited for the Shift Leader to radio me the signal that indicated all agents had returned to the follow-car, ready to roll.

"All Clear," Settler announced. At that moment I gave the command to the driver.

"Let's go," I said quietly.

Motorcade arrivals and departures to and from events such as these are the most dangerous part of dignitary protection. It is at these times that protected dignitaries come nearest to the unscreened public. The brief period in which a dignitary is exiting from or entering limousines, or is walking in and out of the venue location is when he or she is at the greatest exposure. Few will ever forget the news films of President Reagan being shot by John Hinckley while Secret Service agents were walking him to a waiting limo, or of President Ford being shot at by Squeaky Fromme as he was departing from his limousine. Each time I entered the limousine as an AIC and announced to the driver, "Let's Go," I realized that my team and I had succeeded in safely keeping our protectee and ourselves out of harm's way.

CHAPTER 6
A NEW YORK SATURDAY NIGHT

Protecting a dignitary in a moving motorcade is a well-planned and time-precision exercise. It was raining lightly that Saturday night as we motored across town to Times Square where Sardi's Restaurant is located. The NYPD cruiser flashed its blue lights and occasionally blasted its siren to help clear the way for our four-vehicle motorcade to get through traffic. Following behind the cruiser was the black Cadillac limousine containing Mrs. Marcos, Van Cliburn, the agent driver, and me. Behind us were the Ford station wagon follow vehicle, loaded with heavily armed Special Agents, and an unmarked NYPD sedan driven by a plainclothes officer from the Executive Protection Unit. Billy Settler, who was riding in the front seat of the follow vehicle, communicated our distance to the Advance Agent, Chip Reynolds. Chip was in position in front of the restaurant, ensuring space so that the motorcade could pull up unobstructed by taxis or other vehicles. I sat quietly in the front seat of the limo and listened while Mrs. Marcos and Van were fondly recalled the opera. Only the driver and I could hear our radio transmissions through our earpieces. The only other sound was the intermittent rhythm of wiper blades clearing the light raindrops from the windshield. When we were ten minutes away from Sardi's, Settler radioed to the advance agent:

"Reynolds . . . this is Settler . . . ten mics." (code for 'minutes) "Settler from Reynolds . . . (radio squelch) . . . Roger that. All clear."

Five minutes later the Shift Leader called again. "Reynolds . . . Settler . . . five mics," and again, "Reynolds from Settler . . . two mics." At two minutes out, the advance agent must communicate an "all clear" to the AIC. Without that signal, the AIC will not allow the motorcade to arrive at the intended destination. I would have instructed the driver to keep moving if I hadn't heard the "all clear" from the advance agent.

"Schenck, this is Reynolds . . . all clear . . . you're clear for arrival," and moments later,

"Schenck from Reynolds . . . I have visual. Watch for me at curbside."

"Roger . . . Reynolds." I turned to Mrs. Marcos and said, "We're here, Ma'am."

As the motorcade slowed, agents jumped out from the follow vehicle and trotted up along each side of the moving limousine. The advance agent stood with his right arm and hand fully extended, looking at the approaching limo, thus showing the driver where to stop. Just soon as the limo pulled up Chip positioned himself near the right rear door and looked outward. Five agents now surrounded the limo. Mrs. Marcos, Van Cliburn, the driver, and I remained inside the limo, with doors locked. The front entrance of Sardi's had an awning protruding over the sidewalk. People gathered on either side of the entrance, curious to see who would be exiting from the limousine. Pedestrians, who had been walking in the direction of the restaurant, started running enticed at seeing the arriving motorcade. They wanted to observe whoever stepped out of the limousine. Thirty or more pedestrians looked on as the agents kept a watchful eye. New Yorkers enjoy celebrity spotting. For many, it is an evening's entertainment just walking from one popular restaurant or club to another in the hope of seeing an arriving or departing movie star or another famous person.

Billy Settler spoke into his mike: "All Clear." Then the door locks released. I opened my door and exited from the limo. Next, I opened the protectee's door. Mrs. Marcos exited the vehicle, as did Van Cliburn. Upon seeing the two celebrities, the New York onlookers expressed sounds of "Ahh" and "Oh, it's Van Cliburn . . . and Mrs. Marcos!" We escorted the First Lady through the revolving entrance door and inside to Sardi's. The motorcade vehicles quickly moved behind the restaurant into an alley to avoid further attention.

The Philippine Consul General with his wife, along with other members of the Philippine Consulate contingency in New York and one of Van's very special friends, Andy Warhol, joined the party at Sardi's. Andy Warhol (1928 – 1987) is one of America's most celebrated artists. His works are legendary and many of his paintings sell for hundreds of thousands to millions of dollars. Agent Reynolds had carefully combed the restaurant before our arrival and had selected the agents' posts so that all entrance doors would be covered. Reynolds assigned the agents to their stations. Reynolds then led the Shift Leader and me throughout the restaurant, pointing out each exit and showing us the way to the alley where the vehicles were parked and guarded by the NYPD officers and agent drivers. He also introduced Settler and me to the manager. Then, Reynolds departed for the 21 Club to conduct the next Advance. Now it was up to Settler to lead us out of the restaurant via the pre-selected route in the event of a need to evacuate. For the next two hours, the First Lady and her guests relaxed and enjoyed excellent food and mutual friendship while we stood watch.

The Marcos party was seated at several tables in a corner to the rear of the restaurant and out of view of most of the other diners. I perched myself on a bar stool at one end of the small, eight-stool bar within fifteen feet of the First Lady and looked around. Ah Sardi's, one of the most famous restaurants for celebrities in the world. Its décor was steeped in deep red leather booths and chairs. White linen covered each table and crown-shaped, silk cloth table napkins protruded from tall stem glasses. Lavish burgundy, velvet drapes hung as backdrops against some of the white walls and as barriers from kitchen entryways. Sardi's trademark, however, was the hundreds of celebrity silhouettes which adorned the walls throughout the restaurant and bar area. This honor was bestowed only upon the rich and famous that visited the restaurant and had allowed one of the Sardi's artists to complete a charcoaled caricature of them. Having one's cartoon caricature adorn the walls of Sardi's was the equivalent of having their handprints on the Hollywood Walk of Fame. Patrons often amused themselves by observing the somewhat outlandish and funny drawings. As I gazed around at them, I saw Henry Kissinger with his dark rimmed glasses and large, bushy eyebrows; Richard Nixon with an oversized nose; Marilyn Monroe with large, luscious looking lips; Jerry Lewis with a big, protruding jaw; Frank Sinatra with cocked, brimmed hat and that famous smile; Dean Martin holding a martini; Shirley Temple as a smiling child, and so many others. "Care for something to drink, sir?" the bartender asked, his question snapping me back to reality.

"Just a Coke," I replied.

"And how's Madam Marcos tonight? Will she be having her usual?" the bartender queried.

I think he was testing me to see if I knew my principal's favorite drink. He wouldn't be a bartender at Sardi's unless he did--an important part of his job. But not mine.

"Hey, ya know, I just protect the lady," I said. "I don't try to guess what she'll be ordering." He smiled knowingly and tended to other customers.

One of those customers turned out to be a real thorn in my side that evening. A tall, thin, forty-five-year-old man, dressed in a gray, pinned-striped suit approached the bar to the right of me. He stood at the end where there was no barstool. His salt and pepper colored hair was neatly combed, every hair in place. His black shoes were highly polished, and he wore gold cuff links displaying the emblem of the United States Congress. The bartender quickly placed a cocktail napkin on the bar and greeted the gentleman, saying,

"Good evening, Congressman. How's everything going this evening?"

"Fine, Kevin," the gentleman replied to the bartender. "How about with you?"

"It's another New York Saturday night at Sardi's," the bartender said. "I wouldn't want to be any place else," he added with a cheerful sound in his voice.

The man placed his drink on the napkin, turned toward me, and said,

"Are you the Secret Service Agent in Charge?" It was obvious that he knew what was going on.

I reached out my right arm offering to shake his hand and said, "Sir, I'm Special Agent Steven Schenck with Diplomatic Security, US State Department."

"Nice to meet you, Mr. Schenck," he said as he returned the handshake. "I'm Congressman Fred Richmond of New York. Here with Mrs. Marcos, are you?" He already knew the answer to that question. Before I could reply he hastened to add, "She's a terrific lady and a real advocate for New York's arts and nightlife."

"I'm well aware of that, Sir. We've just came from the Met, and we'll be nightclubbing after we finish here."

The Congressman's initially friendly demeanor suddenly turned stern and critical.

"Mr. Schenck, I must say I am appalled by the way some of your agents are dressed here tonight. I find it despicable that US agents would bring a dignitary into an establishment like Sardi's dressed as casually as they are. It looks most unprofessional." Richmond was referring to two New York based rookie agents on the detail who had shown up that morning in rather flashy, light-colored suits rather than traditional, dark-colored business suits. I was wearing a navy blue, pin-striped suit. The two agents lived twenty miles from downtown Manhattan and were not prepared with a more formal change of clothing for the unplanned evening's work.

Richmond continued, "I know your Director, Vic Dikeos, and I plan to call him upon my return-to-work Monday and so inform him of what I've seen here tonight."

What I did not know was that this guy was rumored to be the richest millionaire in the United States Congress at that time. He had tremendous influence and knew people in high places.

The night was already growing long and tiresome. Each of the agents and I had been on duty since 8:00 a.m. It was now approaching 11:00 p.m. The minute-by minute alert status that I had to maintain as one of Mrs. Marcos' bodyguards, along with supervising a detail of agents, was stressful enough without the added bullshit this egomaniac was laying on me. I wanted to punch him out. I had all I could do to offer him a polite response. "Mr. Richmond, your point is well taken. I recognize that two of my guys are not in proper attire. That is why they are now standing outside, guarding entranceways. But sir," (trying to schmooze him in hopes he would forget about calling the Director on Monday), "these men and I have been up since 7:00 a.m. without much of a break. The two you are referring to live in New York, and when they came to work this morning none of us knew Mrs. Marcos would be dining at Sardi's this evening. The others and I had a chance to change clothes since we are staying in a hotel along with the First Lady. But the two from New York had no opportunity to return home to do so. I'm sorry their appearance has upset you. I'll certainly advise them of your observations and suggest that they bring a change of clothes into town with them in the future." I had to choke out the words. I hated being civil to this obnoxious bastard.

As I ended my rebuttal Richmond replied in a near conciliatory tone, "You guys have been at it that long?"

"Yes, Sir," I said, thinking that perhaps my speech had served its purpose.

"Well, that isn't right either. Maybe we better see about getting more agents so you don't have to work such long hours. You can't be at your best if you're working that long."

I replied, "I haven't seen any sign that the men are wearing out. They're still very alert and performing their duties well. But I appreciate your concern. And yes, we can always use more help." "Well, I sit on the House budgeting committee for the State Department. When I get back to work on Monday, I'll see where we're at on increasing agent manpower. But you understand where I'm coming from with the dress code thing."

"Oh, yes I do, Congressman, and you have my word that it will be handled."

Typical of politicians, he tried to bow out of the conversation on a positive note.

"You boys take care now! We appreciate what you're doing to protect the First Lady." Richmond finished.

"Thank you, Sir. You take care, too." I really wanted to give him a final hand and finger gesture of my thoughts but chose to keep my career intact instead. We left Sardi's and arrived at the 21Club around midnight. The 21 Club (now closed) was still a landmark New York Supper Club. In the 1970's it also had a small dance floor. The legendary *Bar Room* in the center of the club has been the watering hole of countless celebrities, corporate executives, world leaders, and dignitaries of every order. Located in the heart of Manhattan, the 21Club was the place to be seen. Advance Agent Reynolds met us at the curbside entrance and led us inside, to a large round table that seated twelve. Reynolds made certain that I had a seat at the table, close to the First Lady. After she was seated, I took my seat, while the Shift Leader and Reynolds positioned the other SAs strategically around the club, near her table and at the exit doors. Drinks were ordered and served, a soda for me.

Mrs. Marcos seemed very pleased with the table Reynolds had arranged. She had invited her dinner guests from Sardi's to join Van Cliburn and her at the club. They sporadically arrived until all were present. The First Lady thoroughly enjoyed the music of the live DJ. At one point she leaned over toward me and said, "Steve, I want you to know what an excellent job you are doing. I'm having a wonderful time." Van Cliburn had overheard the compliment and nodded his head in the affirmative as if to corroborate her statement.

Conversation and dancing amongst Mrs. Marcos and her guests followed. Each time she got up to dance, Settler and another agent moved in closer to the edge of the dance floor to be just a few feet away, should someone try an unfriendly approach.

At one point during the evening, the First Lady said to me, "Steve, let's dance."

Mentally, I froze. This was not in the DS training manual. In fact, I had never been advised on what to do if a principal asked me to dance. I reasoned that by dancing with Mrs. Marcos I would be complying with two aspects of my training. One is to be close to the principal should a threat occur and another is to be diplomatic by accepting a principal's request whenever it doesn't compromise their safety. I decided to accept the First Lady's invitation. I escorted her onto the dance floor and we danced a slow one together. "Steve, you are a very good dancer! Where did you learn to dance?"

"In Junior high school," I replied. "My mother loved to dance and when she heard of a lady who was giving after-school dancing lessons she signed me up."

"Well, that was very wise of your mother," Mrs. Marcos responded.

Throughout the dance, I stayed focused on the job and my surroundings. Only two other couples were on the dance floor. The room was filled with patrons enjoying the evening. The 21 Club had a dress code, requiring men to be in coat and tie and women to be in evening or cocktail dresses. My only concern, since no one outside the Marcos' party knew we would be there was to be aware of the unexpected, perhaps an intoxicated, obnoxious patron who might try to approach Mrs. Marcos. The dance ended and we walked back to the table.

"Thank you, Steve. I really enjoyed that."

"Thank you, Mrs. Marcos, so did I." I wondered if I would hear about this later, either formally from superiors, should it get back to them, or in some form of needling by the other agents. The entourage partied until 2:30 a.m. Sunday morning. We then returned to the Waldorf Astoria Hotel where the First Lady was staying, and where Van Cliburn had a permanent residence. I walked the First Lady to her hotel suite door. There, she informed me that there would be no activity for the rest of the day. I bid Mrs. Marcos 'Good Night.' Having been up since 7:00 a.m. the previous day and into my second change of clothing, I was grateful that there wouldn't be any further activities. I returned to the command post hotel room, located just down the hall from the Marcos suite, for a final meeting with the two-night duty agents and my weary teammates.

"You guys did a great job today. It was a long and unusual day with unexpected occurrences and you performed beautifully. I've got only one criticism and this is directed to Scott and Phillips." They were the two rookies from the New York field office. "Each of us staying in the hotel had an opportunity from the time we started yesterday to return to our rooms, shower, and dress for an evening at the opera. Not so for you two since you came in from your homes. Scott, your flashy, bright green suit and Phillips, your maroon sport coat and tan slacks didn't cut it. So next time, wear a dark suit or bring a change of clothing for evening wear, OK?"

"OK, Boss," they each replied."
I summarized the conversation I had with Congressman Richmond and told the agents of Richmond's threat to call the Director. With that, Phillips and Scott got serious. "Are you going to write us up?" fearing a formal letter of reprimand would be placed in their personnel files.

"No," I said. "But I do have to forewarn the Director so he won't be blindsided come Monday. I'll be relaying this incident by telex to him just as I've stated to you tonight, so he sees it first thing Monday morning. Richmond sits on the House Budgeting Committee which overseas State Department funding. So, there is probably some politics at play here because he's making a big deal over nothing."

The two rookies seemed somewhat relieved. The other agents just made snide remarks, referring to Richmond as an asshole. I told Scott and Phillips not to worry and bid them each a good night.

Shift Leader Billy Settler said, "Good night, John Travolta," referring to my dance episode. "If I were you, I wouldn't give up my day job," he added.

"Settler, I'm surprised you didn't tap me on the shoulder and try to cut in on my action," At the time he had been dating Connie Selaca, a strikingly good-looking actress. When I got back to my room, I took off my gun, cuffs, mace, radio, earpiece, sleeve mike, and clothes, and collapsed into bed for a few hours' sleep. I never did hear anything from the Director regarding Richmond.

"Two years later, in 1978, Congressman Fred Richmond (D. NY) was arrested for soliciting sex from a sixteen-year-old African American boy, who was accompanied by an undercover police officer. Richmond apologized, acknowledged his bad judgment and agreed to undergo psychiatric treatment in exchange for the dropping of the charges. The House took no action. Richmond won reelection. But his career in Congress ended four years later after he pleaded guilty to possession of marijuana and tax evasion. He resigned. Later, when a dead body was found in his apartment--a man who had overdosed on drugs--Richmond ended up serving nine months behind bars."

The rest of the protective assignment with Mrs. Marcos in November of 1977 was spent escorting her to and from the Waldorf Astoria Hotel and United Nations building. As the chief delegate to the UN General Assembly from the Philippines, Mrs. Marcos engaged in official UN business sessions and meetings the balance of her trip.

The UN General Assembly (UNGA) is an annual event in which world leaders, foreign ministers, and aides gather in New

York City to represent their countries. The Assembly convenes October 1st of each year and continues for the following eight weeks. Dignitaries visit the city at different times during the eight weeks in conjunction with their appearance time in front of the UN delegates.

On average, a country's representative stays for about a week. Some of the dignitaries remain in New York for several days or travel to other parts of the US following their appearance at the UN. Protection continues until they leave the United States. Hundreds of Special Agents of the DS, Secret Service, ATF, and US Customs are called in from around the country and placed on these special dignitary protection assignments for eight to twelve weeks a year. I did four UNGAs.

The assignments can be long and tedious. We stand for hours inside or outside of the UN building while our principals are attending meetings and joint sessions. In an eight-week period an agent is likely to be assigned several Dignitary Protection Details as various world leaders come in and depart from New York. It can be long, tiring work, away from families, sleeping and eating as we find time.

Occasionally, agents can relax a bit after an assignment when we gather for a "wheels up" party. This event is so named for the off-duty bar gathering of a team of agents after escorting a principal safely to the airport and onto the waiting commercial or private aircraft. Providing we didn't have to go directly to another assignment, we would meet that evening in a pub or the hotel bar for food, drink, and light fun. But such times were rare.

Imelda Marcos – Wife of Ferdinand Marcos, President of the Philippines, from 1965-1986. The author was in charge of her protection during visits to the U.S. *Photo courtesy of Mrs. Marcos as gift to Author.*

Chapter 7

TERRORISM: THE FIRST WAVE STRIKES

July 22, 1968 marked the dawning of modern-age terrorism when armed Palestinian terrorists hijacked an Israeli El Al flight in route from Rome to Tel Aviv. Thereafter, terrorists began targeting US diplomats and embassies. By 1974, terrorist organizations emerged in prolific numbers throughout the world. The Diplomatic Security Service was then known as the Office of Security. This fledgling security service was quickly inundated with demands to provide better protection for US diplomats and State Department facilities abroad. In 1974, in response to a wave of terrorist attacks, Congress appropriated a major increase in antiterrorism funding for the State Department so that diplomats and embassies would be better protected. In that same year the number of Special Agents more than doubled in size to 800. It was this expansion that culminated in my appointment to the position of Special Agent in 1974.

Between 1968 and 1974, with only minimum-security measures in place at US government facilities overseas, diplomats, military officers and US businessmen were being kidnapped and often killed, with one embassy after another coming under attack. Kidnapped victims' lives were lost in part because the US, under the Nixon Administration, had developed a "No Ransom, No

Concessions" policy, meaning that we would not negotiate payments nor exchange prisoners for the release of an American government official taken hostage. Until terrorist and guerrilla organizations came to believe the US was resolute in this policy, kidnappings continued with the unfortunate consequence that abducted diplomats were invariably murdered. Eventually in 1985, international crime and terrorist organizations became aware of the fact that they would get very little except publicity for all the effort and funds which they expended in kidnapping a high-ranking military or diplomatic officer. Nevertheless, US ambassadors in the Middle East and Central America remained prime targets for terrorist attacks. Publicity was, indeed, what these violent extremists wanted the most. The "no ransom" policy failed as a deterrent.

From 1973 through 1980 a series of vicious kidnappings and killings of high-profile American diplomats shocked the world. These deadly events signaled the coming of age of the first generation of international terrorists. Defending the thousands of American diplomats and staff in dangerous, far-away places (Kabul, Beirut, San Salvador) was no routine affair compared to protecting dignitaries at home. Every Foreign Service Officer of the State Department assumed a price on their head, no matter whether the attack was carried out by transnational, state-sponsored terrorists, or freelance, mercenary assassins (Carlos the Jackal). Terrorists killed four US ambassadors during this period. I have included a summary of terrorist attacks against the US diplomatic community.

Accounts of US diplomats killed from 1973 - 2016

March 1973: Eight men of the Black September Organization seized the Saudi Arabian Embassy in Khartoum, Sudan, where US Ambassador Cleo Noel and his Deputy Chief of Mission (DCM) George Moore were holding meetings. A Jordanian charge and the Saudi ambassador were also held as hostages. Many other diplomats in attendance were able to escape. The terrorists demanded the release of 60 Palestinians held in Jordan-specifically, all Arab women detained in Israel, Sirhan Sirhan (assassin of Robert Kennedy), and imprisoned members of the Baader-Meinhof gang in Germany. When negotiations proved futile, the terrorists executed Ambassador Noel, DCM Moore and a Belgian charge.

June 02, 1973: US military adviser, Lieutenant Colonel Lewis Hawkins was shot to death in Teheran, Iran by two gunmen believed to be members of a radical, leftist guerrilla group. Lt. Col. Lewis was a military attaché assigned to the US Embassy in Teheran.

March 24, 1974: John S. Patterson, US Vice Consul, was kidnapped in Hermosillo, Mexico by an alleged group calling itself the "People's Liberation Army of Mexico." A ransom note demanding $500,000 was received from the group on the day of the abduction. Patterson's body was discovered in a creek bed near Hermosillo on July 7, 1974.

August 19, 1974: The US Ambassador to Nicosia, Cyprus, Rodger Davies, was killed when Cypriot demonstrators fired shots at the ambassador's office.

December 27, 1974: Eight Sandinista National Liberation Front (FSLN) members invaded a private home where a party was being held in honor of US Ambassador Turner B. Shelton. Ambassador Shelton had already departed. Twenty-five hostages were seized. Four people were killed in the initial assault.

February 26, 1975: John P. Egan, the US Consular Agent in Córdoba, Argentina, was kidnapped from his home by twelve members of the Montanaro's. The kidnappers demanded the release of four imprisoned comrades. The Colombian government refused to negotiate. Forty-eight hours later Egan was murdered.

December 23, 1975: Richard Welch, *S*pecial Assistant to the US Ambassador in Athens, Greece, was assassinated by three unidentified assailants. It was presumed that Welch was the CIA Station Chief in Athens.

June 16, 1976: In Beirut, Lebanon, US Ambassador Francis E. Meloy, Jr., Economic Attaché Robert O. Waring, and the ambassador's driver and bodyguard were assassinated by terrorists. The three were traveling from West to East Beirut when they were stopped at a roadblock, which had initially signaled them to pass. The three were first taken to a nearby Popular Front for the Liberation of Palestine (PFLP) cell headquarters. There they disappeared. Their bodies were discovered the next day in another section of Beirut.

February 14, 1979: The US Ambassador to Afghanistan, Adolph Dubs, was kidnapped while riding in his official car. It was stopped by a group of Muslim opponents of the government. Dubs was held hostage in a hotel room while the kidnappers demanded that the Afghan government release three persons recently arrested. Police shot their way into the hotel room in an attempt to rescue the ambassador, but Dubs was killed in the crossfire between the kidnappers and police.

September 11, 2012: US Ambassador Christopher Stevens, Information Management Officer Sean Smith, and DS security contractors Tyrone Woods and Glen Doherty were killed. Several security officers were wounded in an attack on the US Consulate in Benghazi, Libya.

From 1973 to1980 a total of 63 private Americans, 13 American military officers, 2 other American government officials died as a result of terrorism. (*Lethal Terrorist Actions Against Americans 1973-1985,* Threat Analysis Division, Diplomatic Security Service, Bureau of Diplomatic Security, US Department of State).

Throughout this wave of violence in our diplomatic history, US embassies became the favorite target of terrorist organizations. There were many bombings in and around embassy buildings in foreign countries and strafing of embassy walls. In November 1979, the US Embassy in Teheran was stormed by hundreds of armed demonstrators loyal to the Ayatollah Khomeini regime. Ultimately, 52 American diplomats and staff (including two DS Security Officers) were taken hostage and held in captivity 444 days. Their release was negotiated without the loss of any lives, though several had been badly beaten and tortured.

In 1985, after more than a decade of attacks, the DS went through another expansion, emerging as its own bureau within the Department of State. The Bureau of Diplomatic Security currently has nearly three thousand Special Agents, Security Officers, technicians, Special Investigators, and contractors serving throughout the world. The agency is known as the law enforcement and security arm for the US State Department. More than six hundred DS agents are assigned to over one hundred fifty foreign posts where they advise the ambassadors on all security related matters. The result has been a significant reduction in attacks and little loss of life.

Overseas, a DS Special Agent (SA) wears the title of Regional Security Officer (RSO). The RSO protects personnel and buildings by managing a complex and diverse security system. This system includes specially trained units of US Marines known as Marine

Security Guards (MSGs) stationed inside each embassy and a brigade of a foreign city's local police guards stationed outside. The RSO analyzes information gathered from all Intelligence sources. DS Technical Security Specialists install and maintain sophisticated electronic surveillance equipment at each foreign post. RSOs manage an arsenal of weapons and provide defensive and self-protection training to embassy personnel. Teams of DS specialists, bomb experts, firearms instructors, and Special Agents travel throughout the world, assigned to posts where the threats of attack, kidnappings, or assassinations are particularly high. All of this activity is ultimately managed by the Bureau of Diplomatic Security in Washington, D.C., where a 24/7, highly sophisticated, and highly classified Security Command Operations Center maintains contact with every DS representative and every State Department post and embassy throughout the world.

CHAPTER 8

GUNS, BOMBS, SECRETS

Qualifying for a career in the DS is tough, and the competition is intense. Less than three percent of those who apply are selected to become a Special Agent of the Diplomatic Security Service. Once accepted, DS agents undergo five months of comprehensive basic training at a DS training facility and other military and other government facilities. I was partially trained at CIA and US naval facilities. Agents are trained in dignitary protection techniques, criminal law, criminal and background investigation procedures, firearms use, defensive driving, and First Aid. Later, in preparation for an overseas assignment as a Regional Security Officer (RSO), agents are trained in security management, embassy operations, counterintelligence, hostage negotiations, courier operations, and electronic security. Other specialist instruction includes advanced firearms techniques, explosive devices detection, arson investigations, and rendering triage medical assistance. DS agents are armed and have arrest authority. Successful trainees must qualify in the use of firearms and hand-to-hand combat during training and throughout their careers. Agents protect cabinet-level foreign dignitaries visiting the US, protecting an average of over four hundred foreign dignitaries and their families each year. It is our government's way of preventing a tragedy of historic proportion by guarding against the assassination or kidnapping of a world leader while on American soil.

In February of 1979, at the age of thirty-two, I received a new assignment and job description as Regional Security Officer. The State Department assigned me to the US Embassy in El Salvador. My orders dictated four months of language and culture training before consummating an arrival date of June 1979. It was to be my first overseas post after having served nearly six years. The Diplomatic Security Service is unique from other federal law enforcement and security agencies in that its agents are tasked with two very different jobs during their careers, previously described in the Introduction. My first job title was Special Agent. To reiterate, my job as a SA involved dignitary protection, passport/visa fraud investigations, and personnel security and suitability investigations. My other job—that of a Regional Security Officer II— was significantly different. RSOs are in charge of all security matters at a US embassy.

In preparation for becoming an RSO, one must attend two training schools: a six-week seminar, which I had attended in April to May of 1978, and the Foreign Service Institute (FSI), attended from April to June 1979. FSI prepares a trainee to become fluent in the language of the country he is assigned. Allow me to first describe FSI and then provide you with the details of my training at the RSO School.

During my training, the Foreign Service Institute was located in Arlington, Virginia, across the Potomac River from Washington, D.C. It was in a tightly guarded, high-rise office building. FSI is the federal government's primary language training institution for officers and support personnel in the US Foreign Service. Many other governmental agencies rely on Foreign Service Institute to train personnel who are going to overseas positions for their agencies. An agent completes intensified language and culture training (in my case, Spanish and Central American culture studies.) The institute hires linguists from all over the world, most who have gained US citizenship but who grew up speaking the native language of their country of origin. FSI teaches over 70 foreign languages to more than 50,000 enrollees a year. Its class registry lists 450 courses.

Though I was scheduled to attend sixteen weeks of training at FSI, my training was cut short by four weeks. The security situation for the ambassador, the US embassy, and its staff in El Salvador was growing worse due to political unrest between the government and wealthy landowners on the Right and the university students, urban and rural poor on the Left. The Left, backed by Communists, including Castro in Cuba and the Soviet Union, had organized ragtag armies and terrorist groups. They were attacking outlying military posts and foreign embassies. Kidnappings for ransom were occurring. Targets included Salvadoran politicians, foreign emissaries and wealthy landowners. But the most wanted targets of many of these terrorist groups were the US embassy and its ambassador. DS wanted me to get there immediately.

One of my instructors said to me, "You'll have to pick it up (Spanish) as you live and work there. Try speaking the language to any of the Salvadorans who work at the embassy and while you're out in the community. Immerse yourself and force yourself to listen and learn by surrounding yourself with those who are speaking the native language. That is the best way to learn a foreign language."

I attended the RSO training seminar in April and May of 1978, prior to attending FSI. As a result of the superb training, I felt prepared to accept this new and dangerous assignment to one of the hottest countries of political unrest--El Salvador. To me, RSO School was cloak and dagger stuff all the way! It was an interesting mix of security training like none given in any other branch of government service.

One week focused on the proper protection of classified documents. The safeguarding of classified documents in a US embassy entailed multi-step procedures, all of which were ultimately the responsibility of an RSO to supervise. Protection of classified documents adheres to a sophisticated system of checks and balances. I learned that all such sensitive documents were kept in steel, fireproof, four-drawer file safes with security combination locks. A sign-in, sign-out sheet was attached to the inside drawer containing the classified papers. Only one drawer in the safe was permitted to store classified documents so as not to have an abundance of classified documents in any one safe should it be compromised by a burglar or a spy. I also learned that random, impromptu inspections of embassy offices were conducted several times a day by MSGs. They were looking for any classified documents left out in the open and unattended. Classified documents were kept in bright red, legal-size file jackets or white file jackets with a stamped, bright, contrast-colored word across the cover that described the degree of classification: "CONFIDENTIAL," "SECRET," "TOP SECRET," "EYES ONLY." There are, in fact, classifications above "TOP SECRET," which I'm not at liberty to disclose and are only seen by a handful of government officials, including the president.

The State Department imposes severe penalties on personnel who leave classified files unattended. Violations are considered serious infractions in the world of national security. If a classified document was left neglected, the violator received a written reprimand. Three written warnings could mean suspension from duty, while a review was conducted to determine if the violator was still competent to remain in his or her sensitive position. Depending on that outcome, one could lose their job. If intentional wrongdoing was discovered, say for example, a document was removed from the building or was shared with someone not cleared to read it, the offender could be indicted on criminal charges, including felony negligence and espionage. The RSO supervises this entire program within a US embassy compound.   I have to depart here from describing training to relate a huge error I once made in protecting the classified. In my early weeks at the US Embassy in El Salvador, I left a closed file marked "Secret" on my desk unattended while I visited the restroom down the hall. I was only gone for a few minutes. The file contained CIA background information on several of the terrorist organizations operating throughout El Salvador. Upon my return, Gunny Sergeant Steven Saebo and a Marine corporal were standing at my desk, looking very serious and stern. The corporal, who had been making routine rounds, had summoned the Gunny probably to receive instructions on whether to issue a violation to the newly arrived RSO. My new boss, Senior RSO Chris Disney, was also standing at the desk. Immediately, I knew what I had done. It was one thing to learn about security violations in RSO School. It was quite another to actually be handling classified information files on a daily basis and practicing what I had been taught.

"Shit!" I exclaimed. The three of them were silent for two minutes and just stared at the file, then at me. There was nothing I could have said in my own defense, so I kept silent. The seconds of silence seemed like minutes. Suddenly, Gunny grew a smirking smile on his face. Chris chuckled and shook his head. The corporal remained stern.

"OK Steve," said Gunny. The first one's a warning. It happens to many of our new arrivals. But you of all people—"

"—I know, I know," I interjected as I let out my held breath. "I screwed up. It won't happen again!" Fortunately, my office was located in the back of Chris's office and the office of the RSO's secretary. One could not get into my office without passing by each of them.

"Better not," said Gunny. "Next one's going to be a violation."

"OK," Chris said. "Let's get back to work."

Shooting, marksmanship, and safe handling of firearms consumed an additional week of school. DS has both indoor and outdoor firing ranges. One of the roles of an RSO is to train embassy personnel and local embassy guards in the use of firearms in case the building comes under attack. In the firearms training segment, we were introduced to a variety of weapons manufactured throughout the world. We also received more training with the three guns that we had used as Special Agents in the field: the six shot .357 revolver, the Uzi submachine gun, and the Remington 870-P sawed-off shotgun. The revolver is still preferred by some agents and was for years the firearm of choice for thousands of Special Agents and law enforcement officers. In the 1980s' most local, state, and federal law enforcement personnel switched to the S&W 9mm, semi-automatic pistol (15 round capacity) and the Glock 10mm pistol (17 round capacity). The Uzi is described in the following chapter. The Remington shotgun is the preferred weapon for dignitary protection and embassy defense because of its versatility. It has a shorter barrel length, over 14 inches shorter than other shotguns. Here is a description of the Remington shotgun from the Bureau of Diplomatic Security Training Center Firearms Instruction Manual:

The gun is capable of delivering aimed fire with slugs at ranges up to 100 m (approximately 333 ft.). With buckshot rounds, the shotgun can deliver hundreds of smaller projectiles in a few seconds. When used as a tear gas launcher, the shotgun can deliver tear gas canisters at distant targets with accuracy. The shotgun possesses a psychological effect that has proven to be a deterrent in law enforcement work, and in many cases its very presence has caused a de-escalation of force in violent encounters.

The Remington Shotgun has a folding stock that when extended enables the shooter to fire the gun from the shoulder. But with the stock folded, the shooter can wield the gun easily and fire from various positions. The gun has a grip handle rather than a permanent wooden stock. The shooter can grip the handle and pull the trigger with one hand while racking new rounds into the chamber with the other. Because it is shorter, it is more easily concealed under an agent's overcoat while the agent is escorting a protectee. When being carried by an agent in a vehicle, the short barrel allows him to carry the gun on his lap or to wield it into different positions without difficulty, out windows, or through gun portals.   After successfully completing the firearms training course, RSO candidates are certified as National Rifle Association (NRA) Firearms Instructors. This is a distinguished recognition only awarded to the most proficient of firearms users in America by the NRA.

I attended Bomb School for three days at the US Navy's Explosive Ordnance Devices (EOD) training academy in Quantico, Virginia. If there's a bomb threat at an embassy, the RSO takes charge. We were taught various search methods which are used in a building suspected of containing a bomb. We learned about C-4, a claylike explosive material, which can be molded in one's hand like putty. It can be molded flat like a pancake, rolled up into a ball, into a long tube, or just about any shape and size for the intended purpose. Just one and a half pounds of C-4 is enough to blow up a two-ton truck. Owing to its rubbery, plastic quality and high malleability, C-4 can be easily concealed and smuggled past a security station. For all these reasons, C-4 is widely used by terrorist and guerrilla forces all over the world. C-4 can be remotely detonated by an electrical device (or fuse about half the size of a ballpoint pen) inserted into the material. The C-4 is then placed on the intended target. It has often been said that seeing is believing. But I could hardly believe what I witnessed while safely inside a bunker shelter at the edge of a football-sized training field. The instructor had placed a brick-sized amount of C-4 on the undercarriage of a Chevy Impala, which was positioned in the center of the field. He depressed the detonator switch, and instantly the vehicle jetted upward several feet into the air and simultaneously exploded apart in every direction! At bomb school I learned enough to hope I never had to use this training.

At some overseas posts, however, you were it. The Regional Security Officer was the only person trained to handle a suspected bomb. In El Salvador I disposed of several suspect packages after examining them, while other agents watched from a safe distance. Fortunately, none of the packages turned out to be bombs.   For three additional weeks we were immersed in counterintelligence and counterterrorism training not unlike that of the CIA. In fact, instructors from the CIA and FBI, as well as experienced Regional Security Officers, provided this portion of the training. We were taught various spy and anti-terrorism tactics. The counterintelligence training demonstrated various methods used by the enemy to spy on an American embassy and its diplomats. This included a fascinating study of electronic "eavesdropping" devices, their capabilities, and how the "bugs" are planted. Even more insidious are the great lengths that the enemy takes to entice an embassy employee to work for them. We studied methods used to "turn" someone. A "mole" is an embassy employee who is working for the enemy, someone who can cause insurmountable damage to US security and diplomatic relations. Once a diplomat is targeted, the enemy will seek to discover any compromising background information--any skeletons in the diplomat's closet. This may include whether he's married and, if so, whether he's had a secret lover or an affair, a homosexual encounter, or a one-night stand with a prostitute. Each of the aforementioned could be embarrassing at the least and potentially devastating to the diplomat and his family, if the diplomat was hiding these facts. Thus, if these dirty little secrets are discovered by the enemy, they can be used to "turn" the diplomat. If the targeted diplomat has had financial problems, which can easily be detected by pulling his credit report, the enemy may approach the target to seek classified information in exchange for monetary remuneration. Of course, all such knowledge is first sought during the personnel security investigations. These are background investigations conducted by DS special investigators before someone is hired to serve in the State Department and its foreign service, and once hired, every five years thereafter. Owing to the fact that much of the CI training is classified, I am not at liberty to elaborate any further on this subject.

We also learned how to train embassy personnel to defend against demonstrations, including riot control, how to use riot gear and tear gas grenades, and how to organize fire brigades. In some third world countries local police or military may not come to the aid of an embassy under attack. As I was writing this chapter, the US Embassy in Damascus, Syria came under attack (September 12, 2006). Islamic militants attempted to storm the embassy with automatic weapons, hand grenades, and two car bombs. One car bomb exploded. The other failed. A Syrian policeman guarding the embassy outside its walls was killed along with three of the attackers. Eleven other persons were injured. MSGs at the embassy exchanged gunfire with the assailants.

Thanks to the enhanced security program and well-trained Marine guards not a single American casualty was sustained.

81

CHAPTER 9

"THE FARM"

The final week of the RSO seminar took place at a CIA training camp in the mountains of Virginia and proved to be extraordinary. Until recently, this facility was classified as "TOP SECRET." The camp was referred to in the CIA simply as "the Farm." Only a few outside agencies knew anything about "the Farm." Eleven other candidates and I were told to pack our bags for one week--we were going to the Farm. At 7:00 a.m. on a Monday in May 1978 we stood with duffel bags in hand in front of the main entrance to the State Department on C Street in Washington, D.C. Minutes later, a large, silver and black bus with no identification markings arrived and we boarded. We were on our way.

The bus motored out of the nation's capital and headed southwest. After an hour's travel I saw signs for Williamsburg, Virginia. Historic Williamsburg was very close to our destination. We traveled up a mountain road and made a few turns onto far less traveled roads. In another thirty minutes we arrived at an imposing iron gate that was flanked on either side by a twelve-foot-high electrified fence. Surveillance cameras were mounted on each side of the gate. The bus came to a stop and the door cranked opened. One of the instructors boarded. He was carrying a clipboard and looked to be in his early fifties. His graying hair was cut short and stood straight up on top of his head about a half inch. He wore a deep red and navy-blue plaid shirt, khaki pants, and tan leather work boots. The big bus rolled slowly forward and through the gates. The instructor called out each of our names to ensure that his manifest was accurate. All were accounted for. "Gentlemen…" he began speaking rather forcefully, and then in a more normal tone, "…and lady," for there was one female agent in our group. "My name is Sergeant. I'll be your chief contact throughout your stay here. Although you'll have different instructors, you can consider me as your camp counselor. Everything you see here and do while at the Farm is classified, and you are not to divulge your activities to anyone. What goes on here stays here. Any questions thus far?"

I was simmering with a thousand in my mind, but like everyone else I remained silent in order to conceal my enthusiasm for being at this secret, training base. Sergeant went on to explain that the Farm is the CIA's main training facility for covert operations and counterterrorism training measures. I thought, "This is where one trains to become a spy!" I was about to enter the real world of espionage.

Sergeant continued. "Any needs you have or questions you want to ask, see me. This facility serves as a training center for CIA Operatives, Regional Security Officers, and other government personnel who need specialized training in Intelligence, Counterintelligence and Counterterrorism. There are twenty persons in this week's class, twelve of whom are on this bus. None of you are to ask the others in your class which agency they are from or what their assignment is to be. Is that understood?" "Yes, Sir!" we replied in unison.

This meant that the others were training to become covert operatives somewhere in the world—men and women with the same ambitions as mine had chosen to become Intelligence officers for other agencies. RSOs are not considered to be Intelligence officers since it is not their job to collect information. Ten minutes later, we were dropped off in front of our quarters--a brown concrete, two-story, barracks-like building. Sergeant gave us a quick orientation as to the location of the classrooms. More importantly to us, as we hadn't eaten for several hours, he showed us where the Mess Hall was located. Then he announced,

"Lunch will be served in fifteen minutes." We went into the barracks, chose our cots, and headed for the Mess Hall. I attended the Farm in 1978. In the late '80s, former CIA personnel publicly confirmed that the Farm was the main CIA training facility for covert operations and counterterrorism. But the Central Intelligence Agency refused to acknowledge that the Farm was its top counterterrorism training facility. Publicly, CIA stated that it was one of the training facilities that it uses. Finally, in the 1990s, its location and history were disclosed. The Farm encompasses twelve thousand acres in the mountains of Virginia, near historic Williamsburg and the military base, Camp Peary. The 2003 movie,

The Recruit (Buena Vista Pictures), starring Al Pacino and Colin Farrell, depicted the Farm and provided moviegoers with an intense description of what might have occurred there.

The superb training I received at the Farm would one day save my life. In a three-day class dubbed "Vehicular Counter measures," we practiced shooting from moving vehicles, crashing through various types of roadblocks, and performing a maneuver known as the J-Turn. The J-Turn reverses the direction of a vehicle quickly. The driver puts the vehicle into a controlled spin of 180 degrees at various speeds, jerking the wheel hard to the left or right. We learned to use proper speed and brake controls to prevent the vehicle's rear end from fishtailing. The object is to quickly turn the vehicle around to evade a frontal assault and to speed away in the opposite direction. I wouldn't recommend practicing it with the family sedan, however, unless you're planning on purchasing four new tires and new brakes.

Crashing through vehicle roadblocks was an exciting part of the training. Talk about an adrenalin rush! These exercises provided the greatest thrill of all. This portion of the training was jokingly referred to as the "Crash and Bang" course. First, we underwent several hours of classroom instruction. We reviewed the kinds of roadblocks terrorists have used throughout the world to stop unsuspecting motorists and their vehicles. We were taught counter measures used against various roadblocks. The next day we moved to the driving range where we put the classroom lessons into actual practice. On the range, the trainee drives on a two lane, paved road several miles in length. The road winds its way through woods and open fields and contains several blind curves. Eventually, the course comes full circle to a point of beginning.   Each trainee takes turns driving the vehicle while others occupy the right and left rear passenger seats. The instructor sits in the right front. Having four bodies in the vehicle more closely resembles the weight distribution one must handle during a live encounter. All of us wore helmets and shoulder harnesses. Now, it was my turn to be in the hot seat. I started driving at 25 mph as instructed. Within the first half mile we were unexpectedly met with loud blasts from shotguns and submachine guns as if being fired upon! My heart was pounding as the instructor shouted, "Go! Go! Go!" and I sped away. That was the wake-up call. Now, I was fully pumped and driving over 60 mph, expecting almost anything! Another mile and I was told to slow to 25 mph. I decreased my speed. As I rounded a blind curve I saw, 200 yards ahead, a full-sized, windowless, panel van parked perpendicular across both lanes, blocking the road. We had received earlier instruction in the classroom for this type of encounter. The instructor, a crusty sixty-year-old gentleman with a raspy voice from smoking too many Camel cigarettes, and a graying butch cut, recalled for me the classroom techniques we had learned. He blurted out,

"OK, can you go around it?"

"No, Sir, not enough room!" I replied immediately.

"OK, then hit it but use as much of the shoulder as you can. Choose your path now and crash the end of your front bumper with the closest bumper of the blocking vehicle. Keep away from your center front."

"Brace yourselves," I shouted to the others. I had selected the left shoulder of the road as my escape path. The van was facing that shoulder. Keeping my speed at 25 to 30 mph I aimed my right front bumper at the van's left front bumper, and dropped the left side tires onto the shoulder of the road. Now I was driving partially on the road--in the on-coming lane--and partially on the shoulder. BANG! Much to everyone's surprise, except the instructor's, the stricken van spun to the right and whipped out of our way! I was able to speed down the road without any radiator or motor damage.

"That was good," he said with a hoarse voice. His name was Dusty. You just knew that this guy had been there. He had been in the trenches of reality and probably in most of the hot spots of the world in his younger years. He had been a covert operative, but we didn't know for certain whether he was CIA or military. Now venerable and wise and nearing his own retirement, he was training others to stay alive. I took three more blind curves. With each successful maneuver, I felt the adrenalin rushing through my body as my hands tightened firmly around the steering wheel. As I drove, I realized I had crouched down and was barely looking over the steering wheel. I suppose it was a natural assumption of position for someone who had just been shot at by machine guns, shotguns and had crashed into another vehicle. But what came next was worse. Several hundred feet ahead I stared at two sedans lined up with front bumpers touching--completely blocking the roadway. This barricade was set up in a very narrow portion of road with no room to get around on either side. If I crashed into them head-on, I would most probably render my vehicle useless and have gotten us all killed, adding to that getting machinegunned by the 'terrorists." My natural instinct told me to slow down.

"J-turn, Sir?"

"No," the instructor replied abruptly. "Floor this thing and crash right through, and don't let up on the gas pedal!" I didn't have time to question his command. I did as I was told. As I did, two men in hooded masks, and armed with machine guns, ran out from behind tree cover on each side of the road and began firing. Though I didn't notice at the time, they were firing into the air. BANG! The thundering crash sounded like an explosion, so I rammed the car through the center, splitting the two vehicles apart! Sparks flew at us onto the windshield and along the sides, metal grinding against metal, the sound of which was near deafening. The contact jolted us forward, caught only by our shoulder harnesses to pull us back into our seats! There were no air bags.   "GO-GO-GO!" Dusty shouted in a heightened but controlled voice. The forward momentum and speed of our vehicle pushed it through the roadblock. Though the radiator was steaming, we were still moving swiftly away. We kept rolling thanks to the tires and wheels which were left unscathed. A mile or two later we were back to the point of beginning. The vehicle was badly damaged. Concerned about fire, each of us instinctively hurried out of the smoking sedan. A safety crew tended to the vehicle.   "It had to be done," Dusty explained, as we stood quivering, at a safe distance away.

"Sometimes you don't have a choice. It's not foolproof, but this time it saved you guys from being captured or gunned down. A J-Turn would do you no good with the rounds of bullets they were firing at you. It'll be your instant decision as to what to do if you ever encounter these threats while in the field. Our purpose here is to give you as much exposure as possible to what it's really like." In just three days, nineteen trainees and I managed to destroy sixty-four vehicles.

Little did I know then that I would be putting this training into practice to save the life of a US ambassador.

CHAPTER 10

THE DEATH GRIP

We carried Uzi submachine guns on practically every dignitary protection mission. The black butt handle of an Uzi contains a special safety feature. When I gripped the handle, I had to exert pressure with my shooting hand, between the thumb and index finger, so as to depress the back portion of the grip inward. This movable part, when depressed inward, releases a block inside the handle. Only then can the trigger be engaged so that the gun will fire. One must simultaneously depress the grip safety inward while pulling the trigger. The Uzi also contains a "Safety & Selector" lever on the side of the gun. The lever has three marked positions: "S" for Safety, "R" for single-round firing, and the "A" position for Automatic firing. I would have to push the lever with my thumb to either the "R" or "A" position before the gun could fire.

The gun weighs 8.9 lb. and has a folding stock that, when unfolded, allows the gun to be shot from the shoulder. When the stock is folded, the gun is just less than 18 inches long (just over 25 inches long with the stock extended). What a charge I got from firing this gun in fully automatic mode! The Uzi has a maximum effective range of over 656 feet (200 meters). The rate of fire in the fully automatic position is 650 rounds per minute. With the stock folded the weapon can be fired from a variety of positions and can be easily concealed from the public's view by carrying it in a specially designed briefcase or even concealed underneath an overcoat.

It is the safety feature that is housed in the butt handle of the Uzi (the grip safety) that had become a worrisome nuisance for agents assigned to carry the gun while they were on protective assignment in high-threat level situations. Special Agents feared that having to release two safety mechanisms--the grip safety and the safety slide button--prior to firing the gun could cause a malfunction or time delay, should an attack come. A split-second delay in returning fire could cost the life of a protectee or an agent. It was the grip safety that became known by agents as "The Death Grip." For this very reason one agent from the Secret Service had taken to wrapping black cloth tape around the butt handle in order to keep the butt safety permanently depressed. By doing so, only the safety switch near the trigger needed to be slid forward before the gun would fire. Uzis have been known to discharge rounds if accidentally dropped while safety mechanisms are disengaged.   The taping down of the Uzi grip safety by that Secret Service agent in 1975 led to a bizarre and chilling incident. It happened in August of 1975, while on one of my protective assignment missions to the Middle East. I was part of a dignitary protection team comprised of Secret Service and State Department Special Agents who escorted then Secretary of State Henry Kissinger on what became known as the "Middle East peace shuttle excursions." Mrs. Kissinger also accompanied her husband on this particular trip.

Kissinger, Secretary of State under President Ford, made many trips to the Middle East during the period from 1975 through 1977. As Walter Isaacson described in his book, *Kissinger: A Biography,* "Not since Robert Lansing had wandered off for seven months to the Conference of Versailles in 1919 had a secretary of state been out of the country for so long. In 34 days, Kissinger had traveled 24,230 miles on 41 flights."

On the third day of Kissinger's two weeks trip, he left by motorcade from the King David Hotel in Jerusalem and traveled to the airport in Tel Aviv, then flew to Cairo. I was assigned to protect Mrs. Kissinger, who remained at the King David Hotel in Jerusalem. Just before takeoff, one of the Secret Service agents had taped the handle of an Uzi so as to depress the safety grip, thus disabling its safety feature. Advance agents on the ground in Cairo had communicated to the traveling party that there was a large and angry crowd forming at the airport there, ready to demonstrate their hostility over Kissinger's arrival. Apparently, the agent wanted to be ready for anything, so he enabled the "death grip" by eliminating the safety feature. What the agent later never admitted was whether he was responsible for moving the side-safety lever off of the safe position. Once on board the plane, Kissinger, the agents, staff, press, and crew all prepared for takeoff. The overzealous bodyguard, whose identity I won't divulge, took a seat on board in the fourth section, storing the Uzi in the open luggage rack above the seats. The plane ascended the runway in Tel Aviv and headed for Cairo without incident, that is, until the plane landed and the wheels first hit the runway. The landing was just hard enough to shake loose the fully engaged Uzi from the overhead rack, causing the gun to crash onto the aisle floor, with barrel pointing forward. Upon hitting the floor, the Uzi discharged a single 9mm bullet. The bullet traveled at lightning speed up the aisle toward the Secretary of State. As it did so, the bullet first hit a piece of furniture and then ricocheted toward Kissinger. The deadly bullet narrowly missed him, ultimately lodging itself somewhere within the plane. Details of this incident were never made known to the public. Furthermore, the details were conflicting as to whether the bullet may also have grazed the ankle of another passenger. One can only imagine how history would have been altered if the Uzi's bullet had killed the Secretary of State.

CHAPTER 11

AIR FORCE ONE – 1975

Henry Kissinger traveled on one of the three US Air Force Boeing 707s that comprised the Presidential Fleet. The planes were built, equipped, and painted identically. Any one of them could be used as *Air Force One*, which was the designation given to a plane when the president was on board. I considered it a thrilling experience to be aboard one of these magnificent giants. On this trip to the Middle East in 1975, we had arrived at Andrews Air Force base, outside of Washington, D.C., by motorcade on the morning of departure. I was seated in one of the two station wagon follow cars, cradling an Uzi in my lap. We sped through opened, guarded gates and onto the tarmac where the giant 707 was waiting our arrival. Minutes later, I was climbing the boarding steps leading into the plane.

Stepping aboard *Air Force One*, I entered through a passenger door located just behind the cockpit. I heard other agents, who had previously flown on the plane state that Presidents Eisenhower, Kennedy, and Johnson had used this plane. It was literally a command post in the sky.

The first thing that struck me upon entering the aircraft was the huge electronic console and communications area. It was manned by two Air Force sergeants who sat in high backed, black leather seats, and who were relaxing and greeting each of the passengers as they walked through this section. There were phones, teletype machines, all kinds of electronic communication instruments and board lights too numerous to count during my brief glance. It was apparent that these highly trained technicians had world communication in their grasps. Next, I walked through a living quarters complete with a fold-out table, sofa beds, and easy chairs. Then I passed through a conference room containing a kidney-shaped mahogany table.

The next compartment comprised the working area for staff. There were two tables and seats for eight persons. This area also contained typewriters and a photocopying machine. The fourth section consisted of ten rows of first-class seats for the rest of the staff, security personnel, and the dozen or more journalists whom traveled with us. As I looked down the aisle at those already seated, I spotted the famed journalists whom I had only seen on television. Now I was personally nodding to and greeting Ted Koppel, Tom Brokaw, Sam Donaldson and Anne Compton, amongst others. These media celebrities made my first ride on *Air Force One* an even more thrilling experience. As I took a seat, the first thing I noticed in the seat pocket was a plastic bag containing a metal toy replica of the plane and book matches with the presidential seal on the front cover and an outline of the plane on the back cover. Printed on the covers were the words *Air Force One*. Also in the bag were two cocktail napkins with a sketch of the plane, the presidential seal, and the words *Air Force One*.

The flight to Tel Aviv was uneventful, save for the magnificent, seven-course meals served by air force stewards. The menu included tossed salad, hand-carved prime rib, sea bass or flounder, a variety of succulent vegetable choices, long-grained and wild rice, fresh baked rolls, and several choices of desserts. All of the meal was served on *Air Force One* china by the stewards who were smartly dressed in black slacks with gold stripes, white formal shirts, black vests, and bow ties. Each steward wore pure white dress gloves. The flight from Andrews AFB to Tel Aviv had taken just over eight hours. Upon landing, as we taxied to the tarmac area, I looked out my seat window and saw Secret Service and DS agents stationed next to the awaiting motorcade. This team with vehicles and equipment had flown ahead of us on a military C-47 cargo plane. After the plane came to a stop and the stairs' door was lowered, the agents, including me, deplaned first. An official greeting party, including Israel's Foreign Minister Shimon Perez, who had become a good friend of Kissinger's, was there to greet his arrival. I took up a position under the wing of the aircraft. Greeting ceremonies lasted fifteen minutes before Kissinger and Perez entered the black, armored Cadillac limousine for the ride to Jerusalem and the King David Hotel. I was told to ride in the right rear seat of one of the two station wagon follow cars that would be tailing the limousine. As a rookie agent taking my first trip to the

Middle East, I didn't know what to expect. My training would have to guide me, along with the commands of the Team Leader or the AIC. The route we took from Tel Aviv to Jerusalem was well patrolled and guarded. As we sped along the barren, two-lane highway, it was virtually empty of any other traffic, save for hundreds of military and police personnel, their parked vehicles and civilian bystanders waiting to get a glimpse at and wave to Kissinger as the motorcade passed by. Israeli authorities had closed the main highway between Tel Aviv and Jerusalem for Kissinger's motorcade! I was awestruck upon learning this news, but I didn't let on. Everyone inside the station wagon was peering out to see the expressionless faces of the bystanders. We arrived without incident.

CHAPTER 12

"KILL KISSINGER!"

It was customary for Kissinger to stay in either Jerusalem or Cairo and shuttle back and forth on *Air Force One* while negotiating peace proposals with Israeli and Egyptian leaders, principally Menachem Begin, prime minister of Israel, and Anwar Sadat, president of Egypt. These trips were always precarious, to say the least. The general populous of Israel and Egypt both objected to US involvement in their political affairs. To many, Kissinger was a meddler, the "ugly American" sticking his nose into their business. He was consequentially disliked and even despised by some, as was made readily apparent in the following report from the *Congressional Quarterly*: "Kissinger's arrivals sparked nationwide demonstrations by Israelis who disliked his brand of diplomacy and were skeptical of agreements with the Arabs. At Tel Aviv airport, Kissinger said that 'the gap in negotiations has been substantially narrowed by concessions on both sides.' The Sinai II Pact caused Israel's withdrawal from Sinai, mountain passes and returned the Abu Rudais oil fields to Egypt, in return for modest Egyptian political concessions. President Ford asked that Congress approve the new US Middle East role."   The agents in charge of Kissinger's protection during his tenure as Secretary of State were US Secret Service agents, not DS agents from the State

98

Department. Though the DS is charged by federal mandate with the protection of the Secretary of State, Kissinger pressured Congress to amend this legislation so long as he was in his position. He did so because, prior to serving under President Ford as Secretary of State, Kissinger was National Security Advisor in the Nixon Administration. As such he had Secret Service protection. He knew his agents well and trusted them. When he became Secretary of State, he wanted to keep his team of Secret Service agents rather than take on a team of agents who were unfamiliar to him. Nevertheless, agents of the Diplomatic Security Service for the State Department were along to provide protection for Mrs. Kissinger, provide adjunct protection for the Secretary, and to facilitate security activities at locations he attended. Ironically, it was one of those long time-trusted Secret Service agents whom Kissinger had brought along that nearly did him in as was described in the previous chapter, "The Death Grip."

From the time we landed until our departure from the Middle East, there were outpourings of hostility, including massive demonstrations. These occurred at the airports and outside the hotels we occupied during the visits. But the most violent demonstration occurred during an attempt to transport Kissinger by motorcade from the King David Hotel in Jerusalem to the Knesset (Israeli Parliament) building located several miles outside Jerusalem. I was riding in the right rear passenger's seat of the second of two-station wagon follow cars filled with agents, trailing

Kissinger's armored limousine. It was during this trip that I truly came to fear for my life.

Four DS agents and I were seated in the second station wagon. Kissinger's purpose for this trip was to hold discussions with members of the Israeli Parliament to formulate proposals before shuttling over to Egypt. On this particular trip thousands of Israeli citizens had lined both sides of the two-lane blacktop road. Other agents, along with police, had preceded the motorcade and were about a mile ahead. They forewarned us of the crowds but stated that the road was passable. Suddenly, however, as we were driving along, all of that changed. About a half mile in front of us the throngs of bystanders surged out into the street, totally blocking our way! The handful of police in the two cars, which had led the motorcade just in front of Kissinger's limo, was helpless in repelling the angry crowd. The motorcade ground to a halt. In an instant a swarm of people mobbed our vehicles, banging on the windows and shouting angry anti-Kissinger slogans: "Kissinger go home," "US out of Israel!" and "No more Yankees," "Kill Kissinger!" Secret Service agents were in the first station wagon just ahead of us. We were all trapped inside our vehicles. The only way for us to get to Kissinger was to come out shooting! Ahead, Kissinger sat in the right rear seat of the limo, with an aide in the left rear, the driver, and Kissinger's Chief Secret Service agent in the front. The mob began throwing objects at our vehicles. They pelted us with stones, rotted fruits, tomatoes, and eggs. There was little we could do. My heart was pounding in fear, the adrenalin rushing, and I began bracing myself for what was coming next. My chest seemed to be tightening. Then I realized it was the feeling of the Kevlar bullet-resistant vest I was wearing under my shirt that felt tighter as my breathing became more rapid. The feeling of the vest surrounding my upper body was of some comfort. The radios crackled as the Agent in Charge urged us to remain calm and await his commands. He was sitting in the limo and, I'm sure, was discussing with Kissinger what to do. Would I become part of a historic event in which US agents turned their weapons on a crowd of angry but likely unarmed Israeli citizens? Would the AIC signal us to exit our vehicles and surround the limo to protect Kissinger at all costs? Such an order would have meant certain injury and possible death. The signal came.

"Everyone put on your masks." Now I knew: we'd be going into battle. The AIC would not have ordered tear gas masks if we were going to remain inside.

"Keep inside your vehicles until I give the command," the AIC barked. "Keep all vents and air-conditioning off." I reached down to retrieve the mask, which had been at my feet and quickly strapped the mask over my face. I had practiced using gas masks in training over a year before, but I had never worn one since. My fingers fumbled and shook as I donned the mask.

Minutes later an Israeli helicopter buzzed overhead, dispelling teargas onto the mob. Most of the crowd had been standing to the sides and in front of the motorcade. The rear, from the direction we had come, was clear. I turned around and looked back down the road. In the near distance, I saw a long line of military personnel carriers, with headlights blazing, speeding in our direction. Troops were on the way. Within minutes they arrived and began dispersing the crowd, who by now were disoriented by the tear gas and pandemonium. We stayed inside the vehicles another two to three minutes. Then as space cleared between us and the fleeing mobs, we were ordered to exit the vehicles and protect the limo. We did so, surrounding Kissinger's vehicle with Uzis, sawed-off shotguns, and pistols at the ready. With Uzi in hand, I exited from the right rear passenger's seat and ran up to the right rear door of the limo closest to where Kissinger was sitting. I got a glimpse inside of the limo and saw that Kissinger and the others were all wearing gas masks. Stones, eggs, and rotted fruit were still being flung, but now from a distance too far away to cause any real harm. A hurled egg flew by my face, narrowly missing me and crashing into the door window closest to the Secretary. Thank God it hadn't been a hand grenade. Tomatoes and rotted fruit fell from above and splattered on the rooftop of the limo. Stones pelted the vehicle or fell harmlessly to the ground. Luckily, I hadn't been hit by anything. The gas mask also did its job well.

By now, several hundred Israeli soldiers had arrived and quickly cleared the mob to within a safe distance so that we could proceed. Another ten minutes passed before we were ordered back inside the vehicles and could remove our gas masks. Finally, we moved on, arriving at the Knesset without further incident. Kissinger exited the limo and calmly greeted his welcoming party, then strolled inside the building as if he had just come from an enjoyable ride through the countryside.

CHAPTER 13

AT THE KING DAVID HOTEL WITH AN IRRITATING MAN

Kissinger and his wife Nancy, who sometimes accompanied the Secretary on these peace missions, preferred to stay at the famed King David Hotel in the heart of downtown Jerusalem. The King David Hotel is the most prestigious hotel in Israel, having been the choice of many notable visitors to Jerusalem, including Winston Churchill, other world leaders, and movie stars. It is also popular with Israeli government guests and is used for state ceremonies. The elegant and spacious lobby reflects the classic splendor of the bygone 1930s colonial era.

At the King David, Kissinger had a favorite masseur who stayed at the hotel round the clock when Kissinger was in residence, should the Secretary desire a massage. As told in Isaacson's book, *Kissinger, a Biography,* the political views shared with Kissinger by his masseur at the King David Hotel summed up the emotions of many Israelis: "Steve Strauss, Kissinger's masseur at the King David Hotel, told Kissinger he was praying for his success. 'We must have peace,' he said. 'I would give up ten years of my life for peace.'

'How many kilometers would you give up in the Golan Heights for peace?' Kissinger inquired.

'Give up? Kilometers? On the Golan? You must be crazy!

Nothing! Not a millimeter!'

'Then I should break off the talks?' replied Kissinger. 'Absolutely not,' said the masseur. 'I would give up ten years of my life for peace.'

Kissinger shuttled between Israel and Egypt several times over the next two weeks while Mrs. Kissinger remained in Jerusalem. My general assignment called for me to be part of the agent team that would remain in Jerusalem the first week to guard Mrs. Kissinger. The Kissingers occupied the presidential suite located on the sixth floor of the hotel. The agents, accompanying press corps and aides, stayed at the hotel too, although the sixth floor was strictly off limits, except for the agents on guard, and specially invited guests. It felt surreal--having been in the State Department for just over one year and never having traveled to the Middle East--to be staying in the famous hotel in the heart of Jerusalem in the midst of all the political unrest. The view from my fourth story window of the King David Hotel made me think I was in an armed fortress. In fact, I was. Israeli soldiers had completely road-blocked the street in front of the hotel from either direction and were checking every vehicle and pedestrian before allowing them to proceed. Arriving taxis were thoroughly inspected, as were all commercial and private vehicles.

From my hotel window, I viewed the street immediately in front of the entrance. Lined up on each side of the street were Armored Personnel Carriers, jeeps mounted with machine guns, and police vehicles. Dozens of armed soldiers and police were standing guard. Kissinger's all black, bulletproof Cadillac limousine, and the agents' chase vehicles--two armor-plated, bullet-resistant, five-passenger, 1975 black Buick station wagons--were lined up in front of the main entrance to the hotel just a few feet from the door. Special Agents from the US Secret Service guarded the motorcade. They stood at the ready continuously, whether there was a scheduled departure upcoming or just in case Kissinger wanted to make an unscheduled visit. Then too, the readied motorcade was parked there as an escape transport should the hotel come under attack.

Protection inside the hotel was just as formidable. Mounted on the interior walls next to each of the windows were heavy cranks. When turned, they lowered steel shutters to completely cover the window's exterior. These were known as grenade shutters. There were agents and soldiers standing guard in the lobby at every entrance and on every floor. Many of the agents carried Uzis or had them in their rooms, along with their handguns. The Secret Service and State Department agents had separate Command Centers (CC)--hotel rooms located on the same floor as the Kissinger's suite. Each CC was filled with sophisticated radios, teletype machines, chalkboards, desks, wall map, and a closet full of heavy weapons and ammo.

One evening, while manning my post in the Command Center, I received a visit from a member of the highly respected Israeli

Security Service known as Shin Bet. Shin Bet provides protection to Israel's highest level of government leaders and, as such, is the elite investigative and counterterrorism unit of the Israeli government. Shin Bet had provided a detail of its agents to accompany the Secret Service and DS during Kissinger's visit. These brave, battle-hardened men had encountered terrorists and assassins repeatedly over the years. Their reputation as the best trained, most experienced counterterrorism and bodyguard protection organization in the world is indisputable. The agents of Shin Bet live with terrorist threats on a near daily basis. They are regularly engaged in protection assignments, which include specific threats against their protectees. Most Secret Service and some Diplomatic Security Special Agents may complete an entire career without a single attack or assassination upon the dignitaries they protect. Not so with the Shin Bet agents.

The Shin Bet accompanied us everywhere, and I considered it an honor to work in their presence. The Shin Bet agent introduced himself to me:

"I am Benjamin, how's it going?" he said in a brogue that clearly indicated he spoke English only as a second language. He wore a khaki-colored outfit comprised of a bush jacket and trousers. A gold neck chain with a Star of David medallion hung from his deeply tanned neck. He stood six feet tall and had dark black hair and eye brows. He was thin but muscular. His glance gave the impression that he was nervous or anxious.

"It is a pleasure to meet you. I'm Steven. Call me Steve. It's going fine. Thanks very much for all of your support."   "No problem," he replied. "We are grateful for Mr. Kissinger's efforts and for the support of the United States."

"Would you like a Coke . . . 7UP?" I offered. "Please, sit down." I gestured to a comfortable hotel room chair near the desk at which I had been seated. Benjamin accepted a Coke and sat down. He seemed to relax a little, took a sip of Coke, and said, "My supervisor sent me to deliver a formal complaint." Acting most concerned, I immediately picked up a pen and moved a yellow legal pad in front of me in order to begin taking notes.   "My chief (Shin Bet's equivalent of Agent in Charge) respectfully requests your assistance in stopping Mr. Kennerly from committing acts which violate security procedures in the hotel. Shin Bet agents on guard on the sixth floor are complaining to the chief that they have had to challenge Mr. Kennerly on several occasions because he doesn't follow security procedures."

Presidential White House photographer David Kennerly was a favorite of both President Ford and Dr. and Mrs. Kissinger. His renowned candid photographs appeared in many world newspapers and magazines. Kennerly had freedom to roam the White House and to be near the president and Secretary of State at all times. Benjamin continued:

"Mr. Kennerly has attempted to bring individuals onto the floor who do not have the proper security credentials. He brings local press people and acquaintances of his onto the floor to meet the Kissingers or just to see the activity."

"I understand," I replied with sincere concern. "Is there anything else?"

"Yes," replied Benjamin. "Mr. Kennerly persists in challenging our authority, stating he has complete access, as does anyone in his company. He is a very irritating man. Earlier today, Mr. Kennerly attempted to get a foreign journalist without a security clearance onto the floor. Our agents challenged the man, but he stated that he was invited by Mr. Kennerly, so he refused to leave. We had to physically remove the individual from the floor. My chief asks that your chief instruct Mr. Kennerly to abide by our security procedures."

"I will pass this information to my chief immediately, Benjamin. Tell him, please, that we deeply regret any inconvenience or concern this action has caused your agents. We will do our best to get Mr. Kennerly to conform to proper security procedures."

I assured the agent that his complaint had been duly noted and that all information would be passed on to my superiors who would speak to Kennerly. I thanked him for bringing the matter to our attention and for the courteous manner with which he presented his complaint. We shook hands. Benjamin departed.   Kennerly had caused Shin Bet to become very irritated with him. It wasn't the first time foreign agents have complained about him. David Kennerly is a brilliant photographer. Any official photographs taken of President Ford, the First Family, Secretary Kissinger, heads of State with the Fords or Kissingers, and most White House functions during the Ford Administration were taken by Kennerly. He rode everywhere with President Ford on *Air Force One*. Both Secret Service and Diplomatic Security Service had granted Kennerly the same access to the President and Secretary of State that the agents themselves had. I called the AIC to notify him of the conversation I'd had with Benjamin. I also typed a report of the conversation and left it in the Command Center for the AIC to read. The next day, while I was off duty, I heard that the AIC summoned Kennerly to the Command Center where he admonished and beseeched the photographer to comply with security procedures. Kennerly did so for the rest of the trip.

CHAPTER 14

ELIZABETH TAYLOR
PAYS A VISIT

On my day off another Special Agent, Ken Griffith, and I toured Jerusalem and visited the shrines as tourists. Jerusalem has a history that stretches back thousands of years. It is the religious capital of the human race. To Jews it is the symbol of past glories and the hope of their future. For Christians it is the city of Jesus' last ministry, the city in which Jesus died and was raised from the dead. To Muslims it is the city where the Prophet Mohammed ascended to heaven. Jerusalem, source of faiths and peace, and the world's most sacred city, has also been a city of terror, war, and bloodshed. It has been said that the sword has devoured its children throughout its long history. There have been more wars fought at its gates than in any other city in the world. To walk in and around Jerusalem is to walk over a sea of human blood. Jerusalem has been besieged more than fifty times, conquered thirty-six times and destroyed ten times.

Ken and I toured the Old City and, in particular, the Christian Quarter which contains the Church of the Holy Sepulcher. The feeling one gets while touring the Old City is as if you are passing through ancient history. Just walking down the narrow streets and alleys, never mind the shrines holy to three faiths, one is thoroughly immersed in history. The Old City, surrounded by an ancient stone wall, has a total of eleven gates, but only seven are open. One of the closed gates, the Golden Gate, is the gate, according to Jewish tradition, through which the Messiah will enter Jerusalem. To prevent him from coming, the Moslems sealed the gate with huge stones and tons of dirt during the rule of Suleiman around 1538. The Jaffa Gate, on the western wall, was the busiest of the Old City's seven gates. When I was there in 1975, it was the main gate for automobile traffic and pedestrians coming from modern Jerusalem. From the Jaffa Gate one takes David Street down through the Old City. Along with Christian Quarter Road, David Street is the quarter's main shopping thoroughfare, specializing in religious items and quality handicrafts. The Christian Quarter is a head-on collision between commerce and spirituality. At its heart is the Church of the Holy Sepulcher, the most sacred of Christian shrines. Meanwhile, the nearby streets are filled with shops and stalls that thrive on the pilgrim trade. The Church of the Holy Sepulcher was built around what was believed to be the site of Christ's crucifixion, burial and resurrection, and for this reason it is the most important church in Christendom. Ken and I waited patiently along with dozens of other tourists for our opportunity to view this spectacle. Once inside, we descended down several stairs lit only by candle lanterns attached to the stairway walls. The stairs were made of stone. We rounded a corner and came into a cave like room, small and dark, lit only by candles. To one side of the room was a marble slab, about six feet long and three feet wide. Upon the slab sat hundreds of prayer candles. It was tended to by an Orthodox Christian woman, dressed in a black robe. She was monitoring the donations offered by those who wanted to light a candle and was continuously scraping the dripping candle wax off of the marble slab. The room had capacity for no more than ten persons. Ken and I each knelt on one knee and, along with the others, remained silent. This room is believed to the site of Christ's tomb. A marble slab covers the rock on which it is believed that Christ's body had been laid.

Many people believe that the cross upon which Jesus was crucified lies underneath the Church of the Holy Sepulcher because the church was built on the spot where St. Helena found a piece of wood from the cross. Whether or not the Church of the Holy Sepulcher is the actual site upon which the cross was placed in the ground became a non-issue for me. I extended my hand and arm down into the fourteen-inch black hole and felt what is supposed to be the petrified remains of Jesus' crucifixion's wooden cross. It felt like stone. But the relic had a rough, lined texture so made by the wood timber base that remained after the cross had been broken off many centuries ago. I felt a sense of awe come over me, almost chilling, as I realized what I was touching. My day-off completed and having gotten a good night's rest, I walked into the DS Security Command Center the next morning to receive my assignment. I was advised that I would be part of the team of agents who were to accompany Mrs. Kissinger on a well-publicized "shopping" excursion into the Old Walled City of Jerusalem. The event was arranged as a sign of good will. We would undoubtedly be confronting hundreds of curious onlookers, hoping to get a glimpse of the famed wife of Dr. Kissinger.   Nancy Kissinger was an avid shopper of gold jewelry and Jerusalem's Old City is well known as one of the world's best places to find bargains in quality gold jewelry. It was also one of Mrs. Kissinger's favorite places to shop in the world.

As the AIC briefed the other agents and me about our mission, I learned that we would be in the company of another famous American. Elizabeth Taylor, a good friend of the Kissingers, happened to be in Israel the first week of the Kissingers' visit. She and Nancy had made a plan to go jewelry shopping together on the day the Secretary departed for Cairo to meet with President Sadat. We learned that Ms. Taylor had her own personal bodyguards, along with a cadre of Israeli police to protect her. I was instructed to be one of the agents who would carry the Uzi, contained in a briefcase.

Of the twelve Special Agents assigned to accompany Mrs. Kissinger, two of us carried briefcases laden with Uzis. Additionally, six Shin Bet agents and several uniformed police officers accompanied us. Then too, we were joined by an entourage of journalists and photographers.

We made the short drive by motorcade. I was riding in the left rear seat of the follow car, which was situated directly behind the 1975 black, armored Buick sedan carrying Mrs. Kissinger and Elizabeth Taylor. The sedan had been flown in, as had Dr. Kissinger's motorcade vehicles, by a special C-130 US Military Transport plane. The motorcade pulled up in front of one of the famed entry gates. Before the vehicles stopped, the other agents and I swiftly exited to surround Mrs. Kissinger's vehicle. Once we were all in position aside the stopped limousine, the AIC, who was riding in the right front passengers' seat of the limousine, exited the vehicle and placed his hand on the right-rear door handle to open the door for Mrs. Kissinger. She and Ms. Taylor exited, and five DS agents quickly formed a Diamond formation around Mrs. Kissinger. I hung back from the Diamond and slightly to the left. The rest of the agents, including Shin Bet and the uniformed police officers, fanned out in a circle in order to surround the Diamond. With the uniformed police clearing the way past throngs of onlookers, we made our way through a gate, and suddenly the world turned back two thousand years. I could not believe the sight before me. The streets of the Walled City were aligned in a colorful bazaar arrangement and were mostly unpaved, narrow, dirt thoroughfares. I saw donkeys draped with transport baskets, camels carrying cargo, being led by their drivers, colorful rugs, cloth material, and clothing hanging everywhere. Aligning both sides of the streets were hundreds of stands of pottery, jewelry, haberdasheries, tents, and huts made of clay brick and metal roofs. It was like a maze just walking through them. One could easily get lost without a guide. But our guides for that day were Shin Bet agents.

Our first stop was the Wailing Wall, that historic thirty-foot high, holy monument thought to be the original western wall of King Herod's temple and for centuries the principal place of Jewish pilgrimage. At the Wall, Mrs. Kissinger was a picture of grace and decorum, her head and hair covered by a black scarf, her head bowed. After several minutes, we walked onward into the crowded streets filled with merchants, goods, people, animals, and . . . unforeseen dangers. Tourists from around the world, as well as locals, had emerged upon the walled city to engage in this ancient and immensely popular custom of commercial trade.

I was told by one of the Shin Bet agents that Palestinians, Jews, Christians, and Moslems all coexist here as merchants and citizens. They interact peacefully with one another, helping each other in retail endeavors. They visit, argue, but seemingly all got along. What a sharp contrast, I thought, to the world's view of rivalry and hatred that exists between them.

My eyes were trained on the crowd and the onlookers. As we walked along and stopped at the various booths and tents, I glanced up and down the streets, peered into the tents and huts and looked behind the tables at each booth where this "dynamic duo" was shopping. I never did see what they purchased. However, later, I heard that the spending spree that day totaled somewhere in the vicinity of $40,000 US between the two of them (and remember this is 1975), but that Ms. Taylor far out-purchased Mrs. Kissinger. This gave the press little to criticize. The shopping trip was otherwise uneventful from a security perspective, though memorable for the reasons already stated.

It was now the eleventh day of the two-week trip. Secretary of State Kissinger wasn't due back to Jerusalem for two more days. Mrs. Kissinger spent the days quietly around the hotel, or at the pool, or in her room. She was an avid reader, spending hours with a good book, often near the pool, sun tanning. Ms. Taylor had left Jerusalem the day after the two had gone shopping.

On the morning of the thirteenth day into this shuttle mission I began to feel the excitement that was generating in anticipation of the Secretary of State's return to Jerusalem and to the King David Hotel. We had heard that the talks in Egypt had gone well and that the Secretary was in a jubilant mood. The plan called for Mrs. Kissinger to be positioned in front of the hotel to greet her husband at the arrival of his motorcade. I was assigned to the hotel lobby to watch for any possible threat that might come from that direction. The motorcade pulled up in front of the hotel with agents, military personnel, and policemen scurrying into the street to surround the armored limo. Once all of us were in position the AIC opened the right rear door and Kissinger stepped out. Perhaps fifty onlookers, including local politicians, consulate officials and hotel guests, applauded and cheered. Kissinger waved, gave his wife a kiss on the lips, and then they walked hand in hand into the hotel directly past me. They proceeded to the suite by elevator, their every step flanked by agents. I remained in the lobby. Tired from their trip, Dr. Kissinger and Nancy chose to take dinner inside their suite. The following day we boarded *Air Force One* and returned safely to Washington.

I was proud to have been a part of the trip that resulted in the signing of Sinai Peace Accords. This particular trip constituted a second round of shuttle diplomacy, which occurred during a period from August 16 to August 30, 1975. On September 4, 1975, Sadat and Begin signed the Sinai II Pact. George Fether ling wrote in *The Book of Assassins,* "This historic event would have grave consequences for the Egyptian leader. President Anwar al-Sadat was assassinated by Moslem extremists in 1981, in protest against Sadat's troop disengagement and peace accord with Israel. For several years, Sadat had been pursuing peace with Israel. Abroad, Sadat was hailed, along with Israel's Prime Minister Begin, for efforts at bringing peace to the troubled Middle East, both leaders sharing the Nobel Prize for Peace in 1979. But at home, Sadat's efforts sparked intense opposition. Anti-Sadat sentiments began to grow in Egypt in September of 1975, upon completion of Kissinger's new round of shuttle diplomacy, and the signing of the Sinai Accord. Arab leaders called the Sinai pact 'strange and shameful,' and PLO leaders called Sadat, who initiated the pact, a 'traitor and conspirator.'"

Upon hearing the tragic news of Sadat's assassination, I wondered how Kissinger must have felt. Was some of Sadat's blood on his hands?

119

CHAPTER 15

"WANTED DEAD, OR KIDNAPPED: ONE US AMBASSADOR"

During the security briefings prior to being transferred to El Salvador in 1978, I learned that security analysts had determined that the US ambassadors in El Salvador and in Lebanon were the two most wanted prey of terrorists--more than any other American diplomats anywhere else. The US State Department's Diplomatic Security Service had, and still has, the responsibility of protecting all US ambassadors. For the first time in the history of diplomacy, the State Department determined that sophisticated armed details of well-equipped and highly trained Special Agents were needed to guard the American ambassadors in Beirut and San Salvador. Heretofore, each of the ambassadors in Beirut and San Salvador were provided a single Assistant Regional Security Officer (ARSO), who acted as his personal bodyguard. Now, each would have the protection of the newly initiated and heavily armed protective security details. I was part of an agent team go to El Salvador, beginning in 1978. By June, 1979, I had been selected to be in charge of the Ambassador's security detail of agents and to be the ARSO.

Diplomatic Security sent a team of specially trained agents to each of the two embassies, along with armored vehicles, an arsenal of weapons, ammunition, radios, bomb-detection devices, etc., all for the exclusive use in the protection details. The State Department's decision was historic in that it initiated the presence of an armed group of foreign government agents in two countries. However, all countries, including the US, have strict international laws against such intrusions. I was not privy to how it came to be that the governments of Lebanon and El Salvador decided to permit organized teams of gun-toting, civilian Special Agents from the US State Department to move about in each of the countries freely. But I give credit to the expert diplomacy carried out by President Carter's Secretary of State Cyrus Vance and his diplomatic negotiators.

At intelligence briefings, I learned that in 1977, the various Leftist extremist groups in El Salvador had begun competing to be the first to achieve the dubious distinction of having successfully kidnapped or murdered the American ambassador. Such a deed would give the victorious terrorist group supreme status. Thus, efforts by the leading Leftist guerrilla organizations to kidnap or kill the US Ambassador to El Salvador were ongoing, and efforts to stop the terror called for our continuous vigilance and well-planned counter measures. Extremists from the Right in El Salvador also wanted the ambassador dead. But they wanted it to look like the assassins had come from the Left. Intelligence officers had gathered creditable information that alerted us to a sinister plan by extremists, to kill the newly appointed ambassador, Frank J.

Devine, upon his arrival in El Salvador, in October 1977. Devine was the US Ambassador to El Salvador from October 1977 through February 1980. Ambassador Devine was a career diplomat who had served in the Foreign Service of the United States since 1948. In the years since, he had served in diplomatic posts throughout Latin America and had been Deputy Chief of Mission at several US embassies. By the mid-1970s, he was the

Senior Office Director in the State Department's Bureau of InterAmerican Affairs. El Salvador was to be his first (and last) appointment as ambassador.

On the day Devine, his wife, Barbara, and his sixteen-year-old daughter Penny were to depart for El Salvador, October 26, 1977, a threat emerged that gripped State Department officials with great concern. An official called Devine at the hotel where he and his family were staying on the eve of their departure and directed him to return to the Department immediately. Devine was reluctant, stating that he wanted to join his family in order to prepare for their departure the next day. It would take hours to return since the greater Washington area was experiencing a powerful thunderstorm and heavy traffic jams. The caller, Wade Mathews, Office Director for Central American Affairs, told Devine he may not even be going to El Salvador the next day and urged him to return to the Department. Devine was told that a serious threat to his security had been uncovered and that it was imperative that he read the Intelligence reports. Devine would then have to decide if he still wanted to proceed with his planned departure. Devine decided to call some of his trusted friends, fellow career diplomats and security specialists within the State Department to help him decide what to do next. One of them, Vernon St. Mars, was a skilled security officer with years of experience in analyzing and appropriately dealing with such threats. St. Mars reviewed the Intelligence reports and then called Devine at his hotel. St. Mars asked Devine to come to his office early the next morning. Devine agreed but told St. Mars that someone would have to cancel all of the travel plans for him and his family. St.

Mars replied, "We already have."

As I was also briefed, that meeting consisted of representatives of the Federal Bureau of Investigation, the Central Intelligence Agency, the Defense Intelligence Agency, the Threat Assessment Group of DS, and others. Apparently, elements from extreme right winged groups in El Salvador were planning to assassinate Devine upon his arrival in El Salvador. They planned to pose as extreme leftist guerillas (who were also branded as Communists). The Rightists were members of the military, the dictatorship government, and the wealthy elite who owned most of the land. The elite did not want their lands divided amongst the populace. The US government plan under President Carter was called Agrarian Reform. The plan called for the landowners, comprised of a mere fourteen families, to divide the land evenly into much smaller parcels, give each segment of land to members of the poor working class and allow them to farm it. A portion of the profits would then be returned to the original owners. But a large share of the profits would go to the working class who had actually produced the crops. There were several Rightist extremist organizations bitterly opposed to US intervention that would do the dirty work of mass slaughter, assassinations, bombings, kidnappings, and other brutal acts against the working populous and Leftist fighting groups. So, they devised a plan to kill the ambassador and make it look as if it were elements from the Left that had been responsible. The Rightists thought that the death of the newly arrived American ambassador would cause Carter to ease up on human rights pressure throughout the region. Furthermore, they thought that once the Left was seen as nothing more than savages, the US would decide to promote the Right's call for strong measures against the extreme Left. The intended assassination would be carried out in such a manner as to ensure that the extreme Left would be blamed for the act.

While all this trouble was brewing, Ambassador Devine maintained his composure, knowing that the decision whether to go or not to go rested with him. His remarks were typical of the courage such men possess. Bravely and confidently, he stated,

"Tell me how to proceed, but proceed I will . . . and with my family."

The Diplomatic Security Service set to work immediately. Under normal circumstances, the arrival of a US ambassador to a foreign post would have been well publicized. So as not to give the advantage to the newly discovered predators, secrecy became the order of the day.

DS swiftly put into place a new entry strategy. The date and hour of the flight was kept confidential. Devine, his wife and daughter traveled under assumed names, along with two, well-armed DS agents. The Foreign Ministry of El Salvador would be notified just two hours before the flight carrying Ambassador Devine and his family was due to land at the international airport, in El Salvador. They would have to hastily prepare the official welcoming ceremony, which was to take place in the VIP lounge at the country's international airport. On the day of the arrival a small but significant group of Salvadoran government officials and other ambassadors greeted Devine. He signed the official declaration, delivered a few remarks, and then departed through a side door to a waiting motorcade. Protected by the two accompanying DS agents and the Regional Security Officer in San Salvador, and escorted by police on motorcycles, the newly appointed ambassador arrived at the American embassy unharmed. There had been no time for news of the arrival to reach any of the enemies who might wish to carry out their murderous plans.

Within two days of Devine's arrival in October of 1977, the Special Agent team arrived, as did all of the equipment and armored vehicles. Accustomed to the presence of only a single Regional Security Officer and a few Marine Security Guards, the rest of the diplomatic personnel and staff were, at first, alarmed by the presence of the heavily armed entourage. The armed, DS Security Detail that accompanied the ambassador had also been kept a secret. Some worried that they weren't being told of new, ominous threats that must surely be emerging against the embassy and the American diplomats. Others lamented that if all of these extraordinary measures were being taken to protect the ambassador, they would become easier targets and therefore in greater danger of being kidnapped or killed. Their concerns were valid. The premise that terrorists will seek unprotected or less protected "soft" targets rather than well-protected "hard" targets is well known by dignitary protection specialists who concentrate on ways of enhancing the protection of higher-ranking officials facing the greater threat. For example, the road from the international airport to the city of San Salvador comprised a distance of a good twenty-five miles. Insurgents had often stopped unprotected diplomats, commercial airline personnel, tourists, and Salvadoran citizens traveling this route, robbing them at gunpoint. A few had been kidnapped and held for ransom. Diplomats at the US embassy had already requested more protection. Now, they saw that the ambassador was being afforded all of the protection!   Shortly after his arrival, Devine held a general assembly of the diplomats and staff in the embassy's auditorium. He explained, in general and unclassified terms, the nature of the threat posed against him, quipping that he felt like he was a piñata precariously hanging in a tree, waiting for the next terrorist cell to strike. He added that having the additional security specialists at the embassy was good for all. He promised that the agents would avail themselves to all the diplomats and their families, and that security enhancement surveys of residences would be conducted along with security briefings to family members. Devine said that, because of the increasing tensions and civil unrest in El Salvador, security here would become the number one priority of the State Department. He was right. Within a few months, two-to four-man teams of US Navy Seabees began rotating in an out of Embassy San Salvador on two-month, temporary duty assignments. They brought welding gear and installed sheets of quarter inch, steel panels on walls, replaced glass windows with Lexan (bulletproof) panels, and replaced doors with new, two-inch solid oak or steel doors, heavy-duty deadbolt locks, and other security hardware. They also installed sophisticated alarm systems at the Ambassador's Residence and at the Chancery. The Marine Security Guard detachments and Seabees built sandbag bunkers at each corner of the embassy's flat roof. Marine Security Guards would soon be stationed daily in each bunker with high-powered field binoculars, tear gas, shotgun launchers, and M-16 automatic rifles. The embassy was about to be transformed into a fortress.

Eventually, US Embassy San Salvador would become a model for security enhancements at other American embassies throughout the world.

During the introductory assembly Devine explained that each embassy in Beirut and San Salvador was to receive a PSD (Protective Security detail). Next, he introduced each one of the detail agents, including the Agent in Charge, Assistant Regional Security Officer Ralph Curroso, my predecessor.

Devine had been in the country just under two years when, in June of 1979, my then wife, Janet, and I arrived to assume my new duties as Assistant Regional Security Officer and chief of his security detail. Curroso departed that same month to become Senior Regional Security Officer in Madrid. I was anxious and honored to have been appointed to the position by Dikeos, Deputy Assistant Secretary for Security. Evidently, I had performed well enough on protective security details in the States and was thus considered to be capable enough to lead one of only two such specially formed details operating in the world at that time. My orders were to protect the US ambassador by all means necessary. I also was to assist the Senior RSO, Chris Disney, with the security and protection of diplomats and their families, as well as other US interests and facilities in El Salvador.

In the nearly two years prior to my arrival, Devine had demonstrated his expert diplomatic prowess by integrating himself with the legitimate leaders of the Right and of the Left. Devine could gain an audience with the leader of the two movements on very short notice. On the Right was the President of El Salvador, Carlos Huberto Romero. Devine merely had to pick up the phone and request a conference with the president. On the Left, Devine was a personal friend of the Catholic Church's Archbishop, Monsignor Oscar A. Romero (no relation to President Romero). Devine's interaction with the leadership of the Left and of the Right was precarious. Death threats faced Devine daily, coming from warring factions on each side.

CHAPTER 16

CALAMITY AND CHAOS

During the next six months following our arrival in El Salvador, June 1979, violence continued to escalate. El Salvador was a country that was ripe for civil war. For years, El Salvador had been a country with an overwhelming majority of the people living in poverty and a few whom were extremely rich. There was virtually no middle class. Prior to 1974, 67 families owned 80% of the agricultural land and crops in the entire country. By 1978, that number had been further defined as Las Catorce Familias (The Fourteen Families). Most of El Salvador's rich cotton, coffee, and tobacco plantations were owned by a small handful of wealthy elitists who had controlled the economic structure of the country for three-quarters of a century.

Not a very big country, El Salvador is about the size of Rhode Island, with a population of approximately six million. But extreme poverty was so prevalent that a movement from the Left had begun to grow (supported by the Communist regimes from Cuba and other parts of the world) to "take down" the wealthy rightists and return El Salvador to the people. Since 1931, El Salvador had been politically ruled by military generals who were closely affiliated with the wealthy families that controlled and operated the economy. In 1979, President Romero was doing almost nothing to bring about change. By October, after several years of dictatorship, he was ousted in a bloodless coup and a five-man revolutionary junta assumed leadership of the government. They included two military colonels, a businessman, an educator, and a politician. They vowed to put an end to human rights violations and restore El Salvador to peace and prosperity. The Carter Administration supported the junta and US Ambassador Frank Devine (1977 to 1980) was embraced by it. The junta vowed to remain in a leadership role only until the people could democratically elect a new president. For a brief moment things looked promising for El Salvador.

A promising future was short-lived. The oligarchy continued to prey on the poor, paying them slave wages to toil in the dirt while the Fourteen Families grew even richer. For many years living conditions had been miserable for most of El Salvador's people. Rains, floods, earthquakes, and volcanoes (over twenty are considered active, more than in any other country in Central America) had plunged the woeful populace into an even deeper state of misery. The people had been beaten down by lack of basic necessities to sustain life while ravaged by the calamitous forces of nature. Many of the poor lived under tin roof huts or in clapboard shacks with plastic tarps. Throughout the capital city of San Salvador there are ravines, called barrios, in which many of the country's poorest people lived. These ravines were formed centuries ago by earthquakes. Within the ravines lay sub-villages comprised of the rundown shacks, all linked together like a freight train and extending for hundreds of yards. The poverty, filth, and squalor therein were unbelievable. The situation today is much the same.

The US considered its role as one of assisting agrarian reform and helping to stabilize the country toward democracy. The effort was concentrated on getting all parties to agree to a division of the farmland amongst the rural population so that many more of the poor could become landowners. Such a plan, if successful, would help bring about an emerging middle class. The majority of Salvadoran peasants and less skilled laborers earned less than $2.00 a day. Ambassador Devine and his team of diplomatic personnel at the US Embassy in San Salvador worked in consort to bring about the reform.

With such deep-seated poverty, it was little wonder that hostilities were growing among the impoverished masses. Leftist political organizations, supported by violent guerrilla groups, were growing more and more systematic and efficient. By 1978, the Popular Revolutionary Block (BPR), which had started in 1977 as a Marxist-Leninist political underground group of about 200, claimed a membership of 60,000. The majority of members were comprised of peasants, laborers, and students. Other groups such as the People's Revolutionary Army (ARP) and the Armed Forces of National Resistance (FARN) had, through Communist influence and training, taken to tactics of terrorism. These Leftist guerillas set up armed roadblocks along the highway to and from San

Salvador and the international airport, as well as on major roadways in El Salvador. Guerrillas used the roadblocks to collect "taxes" at gunpoint from unsuspecting motorists and bus riders. The money went to fund their rag-tag armies and terrorist operations. They carried out numerous kidnappings, often demanding hundreds of thousands of dollars in ransom. Targets of kidnapping included wealthy businessmen, their family members, and sometimes diplomats. Had I or any other American diplomat been kidnapped, I already knew that the US government would refuse to pay a ransom for my safe release. This policy of no payment of ransoms had been started in the Nixon administration. It was the US government's way of trying to prevent more diplomats from being kidnapped. However, American and foreign business corporations had no such policy.

By 1978, kidnappings by Leftist guerilla organizations of wealthy Salvadoran, American, and other foreign businessmen were increasing at an alarming rate in El Salvador; so were ransom demands, which grew from thousands of dollars to millions of dollars. Hostages were likely to be killed if demands were not met. In the towns and countryside surrounding San Salvador, armed conflicts between guerrillas and national police or military units escalated. In the capital, demonstrations sprang up nearly every other week. The demonstrations were organized by political elements from both the Right and the Left. The Leftist guerrilla organizations had the popular support of the masses of people.

Financial backing and arms were supplied by Cuba and Nicaragua, whose revolutionary leaders, Fidel Castro and Daniel Ortega, sought the spread of Communism throughout Central America. But the Right had the powerful backing of the Las Catorce Familias and was thought to have the support of the military generals and the government's elite. Little resistance was met when right-winged parties demonstrated. But violence inevitably erupted when the police and military moved to suppress Leftist demonstrators. Neither side's violent factions wanted US presence meddling in the chaos. Both ambassadors under whom I served— Devine (1977 to 03/1980) and White (04/1980 to 01/1982— worked closely with the Right's high-level leaders of the government and the military, and with leaders from the Left. The American ambassadors were expected to exert diplomatic influence so as to bring about reform.

While Ambassadors Devine and White served under the Carter Administration (1977 –1981), they were directly responsible to Secretary of State Cyrus Vance. Carter's foreign policy initiatives aimed at the establishment of agrarian reform and the improvement of human rights in poor and oppressed Latin American countries.

Agrarian reform encompasses the vision of dividing the land so that more of the people would have an ownership interest. Ideally, laborers and peasants would each own a little slice of land and all were to work together to grow and harvest the crops. The wealthy families who had controlled the land for so many years were to be persuaded by diplomatic means to divest much of their interest in ownership. They would continue to be paid, though not as profitably as before. They were being asked to share in the proceeds with the new landowners based on the success of reform and the proceeds gained from the sale of crops.

As expected, agrarian reform was not very successful. Elements, both from the Left and the Right, seemed to despise US efforts. Death threats to US diplomatic leaders and local reformers came from radical elements on either side. On the Right, terrorist groups were comprised of police and military personnel acting as vigilantes. They would make raids at night and murder hundreds of Leftist organizers and group members. El Mono Blanco (The White Hand) was probably the most notorious of these vigilante groups. They didn't just kill their targets. Victims were found hacked to pieces, or they were burned while still alive, or thrown from atop high cliffs into the ravines and volcanoes below. Other victims were found decapitated, their bodies swinging from viaducts for all passersby to see. This violent theater of terror was the environment in which I had arrived as Agent in Charge of the DS protective detail.

5452 221900Z SEP 79

TELEGRAM

INDICATE
☐ COLLECT
☐ CHARGE TO

FROM	CLASSIFICATION	
Amembassy SAN SALVADOR	UNCLASSIFIED	

E.O/XXXX: N/A
TAGS: ASEC, PINS, PINT, SHUM, ES
SUBJECT: WAVE OF TERRORIST ATTACKS CONCENTRATED ON NATIONAL GUARD
POSTS
ACTION: SecState WASHDC   (IMMEDIATE)

INFO: Amembassy GUATEMALA
Amembassy MANAGUA
Amembassy PANAMA
Amembassy SAN JOSE
POL-2   Amembassy TEGUCIGALPA
USCINCSO QUARRY HEIGHTS, CZ
AMB   DIA WASHIN
DCM
ECON
RSO   UNCLASSIFIED SAN SALVADOR   5452
DATT
MILGP
USAID   1.   Latest wave of violence -- in addition to Sept 21
USICA
ADMIN   kidnapping of US citizen -- set precedents in concentrated
CHRON
attacks on National Guard Posts with heavier weapons

than normally used previously. Five posts have been

attacked in approximately last 24 hours with Galil and
grenades
G-3 rifles, hand/XXXXXXX and a "bazooka" being used.

Local press has begun speculation weapons may have come

from Nicaragua.

2.   Attacks on National Guard Posts:

A.   Soyapongo -- Attacked 0530 Sept 21 by FARN (Armed

DRAFTED BY: XXX
POL:JLee/PB

DRAFTING DATE
9/22/79

TEL. EXT.

CONTENTS AND CLASSIFICATION APPROVED BY:
AMB:EJDevine(in draft)

CLEARANCES:
DCM:RBHoward(in draft)

UNCLASSIFIED
CLASSIFICATION

OPTIONAL FORM 153
(Formerly FS-413)
January 1975
Dept. of State

Telegram, one of hundreds reported to State Department HQ by embassy officials,
keeping track of the political crisis in El Salvador.

Frank J Devine. US Ambassador to El Salvador 1977-1980. The author was Agent In Charge of his protection detail. *Photo from Devine's book.*

Alfredo Zapata, Commander of the local security guard force at US Embassy El Salvador. Zapata was brutally gunned down by unknown assassins. *Author's photo.*

A Marine Security Guard stands guard at one of the corner bunkers atop the embassy roof in El Salvador, 1979. *Author's photo.*

Agents flank Ambassador Devine as he inspects sandbag bunkers at US Embassy El Salvador, 1979. *Author's photo.*

Author's photo of US Embassy, El Salvador taken in 1979. The MLP (Popular Liberation Movement) had strafed the embassy with gunfire and scrawled their initials on the wall.

The Miami Herald

Tuesday, May 13, 1980   *Member Inter American Press Association*   70th Year — No. 165

U.S. Envoy Rescued From Rightist Siege At Salvadorean Home

SAN SALVADOR, El Salvador — (UPI) — U.S. Marines and Ambassador Robert E. White's bodyguards used teargas and a bullet-proof truck Monday to break a siege of White's residence by Salvadorean rightists, diplomatic sources said.

The sources said the Marines and White's bodyguards lobbed three tear gas canisters to scatter about 30 rightists outside the residence, then rammed the truck through a roadblock composed of three automobiles the rightists had set up.

No one was injured as the convoy took White out of his residence in the fashionable Escalon neighborhood of northwestern San Salvador and into the U.S. Embassy at 6 a.m.

The sources, who declined to be identified, said the 30 rightists were all that remained of about 300 protesters who had blocked the driveway to White's residence since Friday.

Robert E. White
... taken to embassy

The rightists accused White, a strong supporter of the moderate ruling junta, of being a communist and demanded he pressure the government to release the jailed leader of an attempted right-wing coup.

The arrest last week of retired Maj. Roberto D'Abuisson, 37, has raised the possibility of a confrontation between rightist military officers who want him released and Christian Democratic members of the junta who want him punished.

High military sources Sunday said key members of the armed forces met over the weekend and voted to demand the release of D'Abuisson, seven other military officers and six civilians accused of leading an abortive May 2 coup.

The alleged conspirators were arrested last week.

No official statement by the armed forces was released immediately, but the source, who asked not to be identified, said the military chieftains agreed to press for their freedom and oppose efforts by the junta to bring them to trial.

Sources linked to the ruling civilian-military junta said, however, the junta planned to form military tribunals to try the suspects for conspiracy and illegal possession of arms.

Article, which appeared in Miami Herald after the author and his team of agents, along with Ambassador Robert White, escaped from being held as hostages. *Reprint courtesy of Miami Herald.*

CHAPTER 17

"CAMELOT...THIS IS DARK KNIGHT. OVER."

Upon arriving in El Salvador in June 1979, other new arrivals and I had received a briefing from Ruth Verdine, the Administrative Officer at the embassy. During the briefing we had been sternly warned that we were at great risk of being robbed at home. Ruth recounted that a few weeks ago Defense Attaché Colonel Gerald West's sixteen-year-old daughter and her friend had been victimized. The two girls had been home one evening when the frightening intrusion occurred. Colonel and Mrs. West were out attending a social function when two machete-wielding bandits entered their home, locked the girls in a room, and stole numerous valuables. It could have been much worse. The intruders had entered an open window and had terrified the girls by yelling and pointing the machetes at them. The robbers grabbed the girls by their arms and led them to a small, windowless bathroom. They had warned the girls not to come out. The robbers then proceeded to ransack the house, taking jewelry, cash, and other valuables. On a more positive note, Ruth also advised us that wealthy Salvadorans were anxious to rent their upscale homes to American diplomats. These Salvadorans were leaving their homeland by the droves. Many moved to Miami to escape the violence and threat of kidnapping. They were placing their homes in the hands of rental managers. Ruth suggested one who worked very well with American diplomats. I contacted Senior Valdez, the rental manager, who showed me several homes. I chose one that offered me an all-concrete, white, two-story hacienda. It featured two maids' quarters, a laundry room, kitchen, formal dining room with crystal chandelier, a formal living room with sliding glass doors overlooking a pool, and a concrete-walled, enclosed backyard. The home also had a crystal chandelier in the foyer and a marble staircase leading up to four bedrooms and two bathrooms. I made a lease agreement to rent all of this for $400 US per month. Later that year in October 1979, I was alone at home. My only companions were the ever-present anxieties I felt living in this strange and dangerous land and my trusty and devoted Airedale terrier, Shale. My wife Janet, who had accompanied me to El Salvador, was away for a week to visit her parents in the States. Shale weighed twenty-five pounds and was four years old. She was typically tan in color with black markings. With a rugged and wiry coat, broad in the shoulders, and with the proud, square snout of a terrier, she projected a formidable and fearless presence. The Airedale is one of the best guard dogs. They are fearless and were used in World War II battles to run pouched messages between soldiers' foxholes, minding the call of a dog whistle. In the short time we had spent in San Salvador I had witnessed firsthand her canine bravery in warding off any all strangers, including snakes, possums, and armadillos. Now, she was lying affectionately at my feet while I sat reading quietly in the living room. Peering outside and into the night, I could see that the sky's expanse had grown dark and moonless. I was enjoying the evening's *brisas calientes*— warm breezes that were drifting peaceably over the twelve-foot-high concrete wall that fortified the backyard. While I read, I could feel the breeze come through the open, sliding glass doors that led in from the patio. As the night wore on, I decided not to turn on the distracting, bright, backyard security lights, opting to leave just the underwater pool lights on. Locusts were busy singing. Their hypnotic song blended with the colorful turquoise lights that glowed beneath the water's surface, making for a tranquilizing atmosphere. All too often, however, no night was tranquil. One could hear gunfire erupting in the distance or sirens wailing as emergency crews sped to another bombing incident.

I had resumed reading a book by President Gerald R. Ford entitled *A Time for Healing*. The book is his personal account of his role during the events that led up to the resignation of Richard M. Nixon and of Ford's presidency that followed. Suddenly, Shale lifted her head, stretching her neck in the direction of the back yard. She began to growl instinctively. I could see that she was peering out into the darkness attempting to search for the cause of her obvious uneasiness. In a matter of moments, she growled again and began barking emphatically and fiercely, leaping to her feet and bounding full speed out into the yard. She charged toward the rear of the backyard and out to the wall, which was about a hundred feet from where I was sitting. I grabbed my 9 mm Browning semi-automatic pistol, a companion I routinely placed within arm's reach, and cautiously followed her. Two men, wielding machetes, were atop the wall, attempting to walk on the ten-inch-wide surface toward the house. Upon seeing Shale charge out of the house on a beeline toward them with me in pursuit, the intruders turned away sharply and scurried back. They wore bandanas over their faces, baseball caps, long-sleeved plaid shirts and shabby jeans. They looked like clownish tightrope walkers, as they held out their arms for balance in an awkward effort to make a hasty retreat. Then they jumped off the wall. I heard them hit the ground on the other side, but I could not see them. One of them screamed out a dire shrill, as if in pain. I aimed and fired several explosive rounds from my 9 mm over the wall. My bullets whizzed harmlessly above their heads, sending a clear message to the two thugs who had tried to invade my home, to rob, kidnap, or kill me. Thanks to Shale, my ever-faithful Airedale, I was spared from being robbed, kidnapped or killed. They had failed in their mission to do me harm.

I let another hour pass before I felt settled down and calm enough to go to bed. I poured myself a Scotch and sat out on the patio. I had turned on the security lights. My Browning semi-automatic was lying close at hand on the table. *How different*, I thought, *from living in the US, where I could call police and have the intruders*

I praised Shale repeatedly and stroked her wiry hair with the palm of my hand. She sat quietly, looking up at me as she absorbed the praise and the petting, grinning as dogs do, with her mouth open and her tongue lazily drifting about. The continuous, welcomed ocean breeze had gently cooled down the sultry October night. I went up to the bedroom, changed, got into bed and pulled the sheet up as I laid my head down on the pillow to fall asleep. I discovered the next morning that the villains had used a handmade ladder to scale the wall. A steep rocky hill rose upwards toward the wall from the back of the property. They may have come from the barrio that was at the bottom, several hundred feet below. Their leap back down was considerably more precarious than their climb up. I reveled at the notion that one of the screaming intruders had seriously injured himself.   The next few days and nights passed without incident, but then came the night of October 30th. I had fulfilled my protection duties for the day, or so it seemed. On this night, like every other night, I slept with my pistol under my pillow and an Uzi submachine gun under the bed. The red illuminated numbers on the digital alarm clock read "9:45 p.m." In ten hours, I'd be going to the Ambassador's Residence to meet my team of agents to plan the daily protective escort to the Chancery. This night, like all others, I lay in bed, waiting for sleep to come. Instead of counting sheep I counted each of the steps I had taken to secure the house that evening.

Shale lay at the foot of my bed this night like every night. As I lay on my back with my eyes closed, I mentally walked through the home, recalling locking every door and window. Had I forgotten to secure any one of them? No, not this night--all had been secured. As I began to doze off, I also recalled that I had set the first-floor motion detectors, which if tripped by an intruder would set off a loud siren and turn on emergency floodlights that were mounted in the ceiling corners. Now at long last, I could sleep. I glanced one last time at the clock: 10:00 p.m. All was well. I bid myself good night and fell into sleep.

No sooner had I fallen asleep when the phone on the nightstand rang loudly, waking me with its startling ring. I picked up the phone and said "Hello." It was Chris Disney.

"Steve, this is Chris. Are you awake?" When the boss calls, you're always awake. Chris was into his third year of what was supposed to be for him a two-year tour in El Salvador as Regional Security Officer. Chris oversaw all security operations for the US Embassy in El Salvador. He was also in charge of the US Marine Security Guard detail (MSG), which was stationed in El Salvador to guard the embassy.

"Steve, get dressed and bring full-riot gear. I'll pick you up in twenty minutes. I've just been called by Mel. There's going to be a march on the embassy by several hundred demonstrators (*manifestantes*). Their intent is to break in, set fires and destroy the building!"

"OK, Chris . . . see ya in twenty." I hung up the phone, sat for a minute on the edge of the bed, then got up and prepared myself for battle.

Chris pulled up minutes later. He had already picked up two other agents. We sped toward the embassy in an armored-plated Chevy Suburban. Chris had also called the Marine House, a large mansion located in an upper-class area of San Salvador, which had been leased by the embassy to quarter the contingent of twenty-four Marine Security Guards. He related the crisis to Gunny Sergeant Saebo, who said that he and sixteen Marines would be at the embassy by 11:30 p.m. Of the twenty-four Marine guards assigned to embassy duty in El Salvador, six were already on duty at the embassy and two were guarding the Ambassador's Residence. Thank God we wouldn't be alone!

The perimeter of the Chancery (another word for embassy) was protected by black, wrought-iron fencing, eight feet high on three sides and a twelve-foot-high concrete wall on the remaining side. Public streets ran adjacent to the walls and fencing. There was an expanse of three hundred feet of flat, grassy lawn extending throughout the interior grounds between the fenced barriers and the building. The embassy itself was a three-story, 16,000 square feet concrete building. Each floor contained numerous six-foot long windows, but only a few were made of bullet-resistant Lexan glass.

A three-foot high concrete rampart rose above the flat roof of the embassy, giving us a good vantage point to take up defensive positions and prepare for an oncoming attack. (See photo.) We arrived at 11:20 p.m. Accompanied by four Marines and four agents, Chris and I went atop the roof with tear gas canisters, Uzis, shotguns, gas masks, radios, and First Aid kits. Two other Marines kept their vigil at the iron-gated embassy entrance to await the arrival of the other Marines. Each minute seemed like ten, dragging on in silent anticipation of the confrontation. Actually, it was a beautiful summer night. There was a bright moon, a multitude of stars, and a subtle breeze barely rustling the leaves of the palm trees on the lawn. Like the calm before a storm, it hardly seemed to be the setting for an assault. Then the radio silence broke. Sgt. Saebo announced that he and the other Marines were three minutes out.

"Any sign of demonstrators, Gunny?" asked Chris.

"Nothing . . . all quiet on the ride up. We drove past the university on the south side but saw nothing."

"OK, Gunny," Chris said. "I'll alert the front gate that you're approaching." Another minute went by and the gates swung open to welcome the sixteen Marines. Marine Security Guards are highly trained for just this sort of thing. They guard American embassies all over the world, and at this moment I was really glad to see them arrive. They jumped out of the transport bus, reporting for duty and dressed in full-battle gear, with flak jackets, tear gas grenades, rifles, gas masks, and battle helmets. They quickly took up their positions inside the embassy and on the roof. Gunny positioned his Marines, three each at each of the three entrances to the embassy and seven others, including Gunny, who joined us on the roof. It was now 11:50 p.m. and still no sign of the demonstrators. Where were they?

At 12:05 a.m. the radio crackled:

"Camelot . . . Camelot . . . this is Dark Knight . . . over." Camelot was a security code name for the embassy. Dark Knight was the code name the CIA agent had dubbed for himself.

"Go ahead, Dark Knight," replied Chris.

"I'm in a 1970 Volkswagen Beetle, driving the outer perimeter. I see torches and banners being carried by what appears to be a crowd of several hundred people coming up Salvador Boulevard, heading toward the compound perhaps a third of a mile away. Do you see them?"

Chris and I moved over to the south wall and with field glasses we peered down the boulevard. There they were. "We sure do," Chris said. "That crowd seems to stretch for a long way. We can faintly hear them chanting."

"This is Dark Knight. I'm parallel to them now on the next street over. I can hear their chants: "¡Salga El Salvador! ¡Vaya Yanqui! ¡Incendríamos Ustedes al Infierno!"
("Leave El Salvador! Yankees Go! We'll burn you to Hell!")

"Dark Knight . . . are you coming in?"

"Negative. I'm in disguise. I'll stay out here on the streets and try to report anything I see coming at you."

"Be safe, Dark Knight," Chris said. I knew of Mel's disguises. He spoke perfect Spanish and had more disguises than the Metropolitan Opera has costumes. This guy could dress to look like a local street vendor, a cop, a woman, an old man, a street sweeper, or just about anyone you might see on the streets of San Salvador. He was extremely brave, a man in his late forties who stood about 5'8" tall. Mel was an Agency veteran of Vietnam. He had been on the rooftop of the US Embassy in Saigon during the famed helicopter evacuation of Americans.

Now the angry chanting of approaching demonstrators and their burning torches pierced the still night, slowly transforming the dark peacefulness into a prelude to violence. Chris stood up and got on the radio to the Marines and the other DS agents.

"OK, everyone, remember the rules of engagement. We can do nothing unless and until they come over the walls. So long as they're out in the public streets, even if they start shooting at us, we cannot return fire or repel them in anyway. You and I know that the Guardia Nacional and the Salvadoran Police must be aware of this, too. But it's doubtful that they will show up soon because they don't want to go up against these hostile students and locals protesting the US presence. This country's leadership is at great risk. The president may not be able to command the troops to defend against a demonstration on the US embassy." Along with left and right-winged extremist groups, the students at the university and many of their peers in El Salvador had grown hostile to America's presence.

Chris continued, "We're likely to be on our own here, but US soil only exists inside the outer perimeter fencing. So, until I give the command, you hunker down and dodge whatever they throw at us."

My God, I thought to myself. *This could be it. If they have RPG rocket launchers (shoulder mounted grenade rocket launchers that can destroy a tank) and fire them from outside the embassy compound, we'll be worse off than Davy Crockett and his boys at the Alamo. At least they could return fire!* The terrible reality of the crisis at hand jolted my whole being. But I quickly recovered, realizing what we had to do.

"Screw the rules of engagement," I muttered to myself. "If the bastards start using rocket launchers, I'm returning fire!"

We watched as a thick, black, monstrous shadow of hundreds of demonstrators advanced up the boulevard toward us. The chanting grew louder and louder.

"¡Máten a los Yanquis. ¡Incéndie la embajada. ¡EU afuera El Salvador. ¡Incéndie! ¡Incéndie! ¡Incéndie!" ("Kill the Yankees! Burn the embassy! US out of El Salvador! Burn! Burn! Burn!") As the demonstrators surged ever closer—now barely a hundred yards from the south wall—we scrambled to put more sandbags up on the rampart protecting our roof. Chris assigned two Marines to each of the four sandbagged bunker corners and positioned the rest of us along the south wall of the roof.

"Everyone stay down!" he commanded. "Don't let them see that we're on the roof---no sense in giving them a target." The radio squawked again.

"Camelot . . . this is Dark Knight (squelch) . . . watch out for those banners. They're wrapped around several ladders. Ladders . . . ladders being carried by the mob (squelch) . . . I repeat ladders are in the crowd."

"Copy that, Dark Knight," Chris replied and passed the information along to the rest of us. By 12:30 a.m. the fuming mob had arrived at the south wall. They were in the street, shouting and chanting. Suddenly, they stripped paper off the banners, exposing the ladders. They rushed forward to mount the ladders on the wall. Then someone from the crowd began firing shots. In a flash we all fell to full-prone positions behind the rampart. Two, maybe three pistol shots rang out.

"Is anyone hit?" I barked over the radio. No one replied.

"Dark Knight . . . Dark Knight to Camelot . . . (squelch).

Mel's electrified voice broke in. "Watch the southeast corner! Ladders . . . ladders going up on the southeast corner!"

"Roger that, Dark Knight," Chris replied. I wondered instantly how it was that Mel could be reporting without being detected. Simultaneously, I decided the "how" wasn't important. I was just glad that he was out there. Minutes later we spotted movements on the top of the perimeter wall, about sixty yards away. A dozen demonstrators streamed over the wall and jumped onto the embassy grounds. They were in!

"Fire the tear gas!" Chris commanded.

Marines in the bunker nearest the southeast corner launched a load of tear gas canisters from their shotguns. Demonstrators retaliated by hurling Molotov cocktail torches over the perimeter fence, the foul fuel bursting into flames on the lawn. But the lawn was wet and the lit bombs quickly extinguished. An underground sprinkler had, by happenstance, just finished watering the grass. The raucous chanting persisted, and another round from a pistol shattered the night air. We figured someone was just firing the gun into the air because they couldn't get an accurate line shot toward us from the ground on the outside of the wall. With field glasses trained on the southeast corner, we watched as a dozen or so of the *manifestantes* spread themselves out on the lawn, fleeing from the tear gas in a panicked state. They appeared paralyzed by the chaos, not knowing what to do next.

More and more demonstrators poured over the wall, falling clumsily onto the grounds. Some of them were carrying knapsacks, presumed to be containing explosives or other weapons. The Marines fired more tear gas. In response, the rioters pulled plastic bags out of their pockets and donned them loosely over their heads, in a vain attempt to lessen the immobilizing effects of the gas. I trained my field glasses on the rioters as they darted about in panic.

"Chris, one of them is carrying an Uzi!" I blurted. Chris gave the command to fire more tear gas. A moment later bursts of rapid shots rang out as the Uzi-toting rioter began firing. We fell down behind the wall but not before Gunny cried out,

"I'm hit! I'm hit!" He was barely twenty feet away from us. Moments later a Marine corporal was hit in the mouth by a ricocheting bullet. He was bleeding profusely. While two other Marines tended to their wounded comrades, Chris gave a command to one of the Marines.

"Take him out," Chris ordered, referring to the demonstrator with the Uzi. The Marine took steady aim and fired, blowing away the shoulder of the assailant. More, loud cannon-like bursts blared from the shotguns. Noxious smoke billowed like a blustery, white cloud onto the grounds below. The demonstrators decided to make a retreat and, in a desperate attempt to avoid being engulfed, began running wildly toward the fencing and the wall. They now used the ladders for their retreat. We heard coughing and choking. In an instant, the demonstrators scrambled over the wall, jumping onto the outside pavement below. They were gone. Then, the shrill of a hundred sirens pierced the night air and we knew that the Guardia Nacional had been called out to quell the demonstration. It was a welcomed sound. As we watched the crowd retreat, we also spotted the reflections of flashing blue police lights speeding through the darkness and coming toward us, closing in from every direction. Demonstrators trickled away from the embassy. The crowd, now scattered and in full flight, was scarcely in any mood to face the extreme law enforcement measures doled out by police in this third world country. Back inside the compound we hastily turned our attention to Gunny and the other wounded Marine. Chris and I rushed over to them. The wounded corporal was all right; his mouth had stopped bleeding, but he was missing his two front teeth. Sitting next to him was Gunny, slumped heavily against the rooftop wall, grimacing and holding his right ear. Gunny's ear was partially missing where the lower part and lobe had once hung. Blood soaked his hand and ran down his arm, but a corpsman quickly applied a compress to control the bleeding. Despite the grisly injury, Gunny was still conscious and managed to mutter words of admonishment to himself for not putting his helmet on.

"At least I'll get my Purple Heart after all," he snickered. The corpsman finished wrapping the head and ear, and Gunny relaxed to smoke a cigarette while the rest of us kept watch. Gunnery Sergeant Steve Saebo was in charge of the Marines who guarded the embassy. If one's image of a classic, career US Marine was a square jawed, six foot-four-inch tall, broad-shouldered, slim waste, and rugged looking man in his early thirties, Gunnery Sergeant Saebo fit the description to a tee.

The wind was now blowing away from the embassy, and with it drifted the tear gas smoke toward the now disbanding crowd. We were finally able to remove our masks. Yet, we kept up our vigil for another two hours. In the meantime, chaos had erupted outside the embassy walls as police, using megaphones and wielding riot batons and shields, cleared away the demonstrators. Police guards were posted around the perimeter where they remained throughout the rest of that morning.

3:00 a.m. We all came down from the roof, except for two Marines in each of the corner bunkers. Back inside the embassy we started making pots of coffee and began putting away the riot gear. How much worse it could have been! Thanks to Dark Knight we had received good information, and, consequently, we were prepared for the siege. I wondered if we'd hear from him again. Mel had instructed Chris never to call him, only to respond if Mel called him first. That was so that his radio would remain silent unless he was using it. By 5:00 a.m., Chris ordered the Marines to stand down and return to their quarters, except for the eight who remained on duty. Chris drove the other agents to their homes and me back to mine. Just as we arrived at my driveway the radio crackled one more time.

"Dark Knight to Camelot."

"Go ahead, Dark Knight."

"All Clear? Is everyone safe?"

"Safe enough," Chris replied. "What about you? Are you OK?"
"Couldn't be better! Sharp as a tack and ready for more!" Mel exclaimed." I honestly believe he lived for these moments. He loved the action.

"You really came through for us, Dark Knight . . . thanks a million." Chris said.

"All in a day's work. See you boys later . . . Dark Knight out." I could tell by the emphasis and tone in his voice that he was pleased with his performance, and so he should have been. Chris and I sat together for a moment as the armored Suburban idled in front of my house. He spoke softly and reflectively.

"What a crazy business this is, Steve. Here we are a couple of civilians with the job of managing security affairs for a US embassy and suddenly we have to don armor and become paramilitary professionals." Can you imagine any other job like it?"

"No, Chris, I can't. But I think you and I, and DS officers around the world, are going to be in for a lot more of this kind of stuff." Every week, telegrams from HQ in Washington bore this fact out with contents of how terrorism was escalating in many places around the world, and more of our embassies were coming under attack.

"How long have you been down here now, Steve?"

"About four months."

"I've been here about thirty months, and it's getting a lot worse," he said. "Threats on the embassy, actual attacks, and threats against the ambassador and embassy personnel are becoming more frequent. The US business community here is scared, and many are talking of leaving or have already pulled out. It won't be long before the whole country will erupt into a full-scale civil war."

It was good to have had this chat with Chris. Until now, we had very little time to just sit and talk. Chris was always in meetings or attending to his other duties while I was accompanying the ambassador daily.

"I know, Chris. We're really going to have to be on our toes. A lot more's coming ahead."

"I don't envy you and the other agents going out into those streets everyday with the ambassador. I pray you guys stay safe and nothing happens."

I could tell Chris was getting weary. The responsibility of managing embassy security and the safety of more than 150 Foreign Service professionals lay heavily on his shoulders this night and every night. In a post like Paris, Stockholm, or Rome it wouldn't have been so bad. But in El Salvador, like in many other US embassy posts where conditions were wrought with crime and terrorism, government upheaval, corruption and disdain for US presence, the threat was ever more menacing. RSOs have the immense responsibility of keeping US embassy buildings and all of the personnel safe from harm. Chris was really feeling that responsibility at this moment.

"You did well tonight, Steve."

"No, Chris, I just followed your directions. You were the one that did well."

Then I tried to lighten the conversation. "Chris, have you been rehearsing for an attack on the embassy in your spare time? You led our defense in textbook style. I'd call it an award-winning performance! In fact, I think you should win an Oscar for this one!" By now I had him grinning.

"I think you're full of it, Schenck," he chuckled. "Better get some rest. I'll see you in a few hours."

With that, we bid each other good night, and Chris drove off. With the remote keypad mounted on the exterior wall to deactivate the electronic gate lock, I entered onto my property. I reset that lock and then deactivated the interior alarms, using the keypad mounted on the wall at the front porch. I opened the front door, dropped my gear, walked upstairs, shed my clothing, and finally crawled into bed at 5:30 a.m., knowing full well that my alarm would go off in two hours.

That morning, like every other weekday morning, I had to be over to the Ambassador's Residence by 8:00 a.m. There, I met the other DS agents, along with two Special Ops soldiers, dressed in civilian clothes and on loan to us for added support. As was the routine, the five agents and I were to escort the ambassador from his residence to the embassy or elsewhere and later return to the residence. On days that we had an advance security report that there was a plan afoot to attack the motorcade, we didn't leave at all. Instead, the ambassador conducted business from his home. Since we had just fought off demonstrators hours earlier, we wanted to make certain there was no imminent threat or lingering tear gas. I called Gunny Saebo, who was already at the embassy after his brief two-hour rest.

"Everything's fine over here, Steve," he said, "save for a few burn marks in the lawn and graffiti on the walls."

"Thanks, Gunny, we'll see you in a while." I told the team we'd be rolling and they commenced to prepare another circuitous route.

CHAPTER 18
MOTORCADE UNDER ATTACK

Some years later I saw the movie *Clear and Present Danger,* starring Harrison Ford as CIA Analyst Jack Ryan. A particularly action-packed and deadly scene in the movie caused me to recall a similar brush with death that occurred in El Salvador. It happened on a morning in February of 1980. Ambassador Devine, who had endured a number of threats and had boldly fulfilled his diplomatic mission, was completing his final few weeks as US ambassador. The detail's agents and I were to escort the ambassador in the three-vehicle motorcade from his residence to the embassy. We had selected a route that would take us on a sparsely traveled road. It was one of the many routes to and from the Ambassador's Residence and the embassy that we had carefully mapped out months earlier when this mission had begun. Each morning prior to departure, we would discuss the various routes and out of the bag of choices select one of those routes, thus invoking the counterterrorist' tactic of foregoing a routine pattern and opting for surprise instead. This particular route took us behind the city rather than through it. The two-lane paved road was usually void of traffic and was quite picturesque. The mountains were in the distance to the north, and one of the few upper class residential districts was situated in a valley to the south. I was riding in my usual position as Agent in Charge in the front right passenger's side of the 1978, armored black Cadillac limousine. Ambassador Devine was comfortably seated behind me, engaged in his morning ritual of reading a few American newspapers and the daily local paper, *El Diario del Hoy*. Agent Tom Fox was the driver. Behind us rolled the "Yellow Monster," a name we dubbed for the follow car, a nearly two-ton, heavily armored 1978 Chevrolet Suburban. It was painted silver and yellow. Inside the Suburban sat two DS agents and the two Special Ops. Guys. Each of them carried automatic weapons. Agent Fred Manning was out in front by about a quarter mile driving the lead vehicle, a 1978 armored Plymouth Fury. This comprised our everyday motorcade for transporting and protecting the ambassador.

The ride through the countryside was peaceful, and I tried to settle down just a bit and enjoy the scenery. Knowing that every day was a day some terrorist organization was looking for an opportunity to kidnap or kill the ambassador meant never being able to totally relax. Suddenly, Manning's voice crackled through my radio. I was wearing an earpiece attached to the radio so that our transmissions would not disturb the ambassador.

"There's a military roadblock ahead of me. I can see soldiers with rifles lined along each side of the road, and a military officer is standing in the road next to a jeep parked in our lane."

I was distressed as to why there would be a military roadblock on this road. I mentally recalled earlier Intelligence reports I had read. However, these reports had indicated that rebels had stolen military uniforms and vehicles and were posing as soldiers in front of roadblocks in order to rob, murder, or kidnap.

"Roger," I replied. "Schenck to all agents: put roadblock counter measures into effect." I spoke into a sleeve mic that was attached to the two-way radio clamped onto my waist belt and concealed under my suit coat. Hearing me, Ambassador Devine put down the newspaper he had been reading.

"Is everything all right, Mr. Schenck?"

I detected an element of concern in his voice. I quickly explained what was happening. "Let's hope they're really military and that they got the message," he said, as he drew a small, semiautomatic pistol from his coat pocket and laid it on the seat beside him. Legitimate military units in El Salvador were very familiar with the appearance of the American ambassador's motorcade. Commanders had instructions never to stop the motorcade. By way of well-established relations with the Minister of Defense and high-ranking military officers, the ambassador and our Defense Attaché had previously negotiated a "No Stop" policy. This protocol or "message," as Devine had referred to it, should have been relayed to all commanders that might be conducting legitimate roadblocks. If the roadblock were a terrorist ploy, the worst thing we could do would be to bring the motorcade to a halt. Manning had slowed the lead car to a crawl, waiting for us to catch up. Our security plan in the event of such an encounter was too slow to about 10 mph but to never stop.

"How many do you count, Fred?" I asked.

"Looks like ten to twelve soldiers standing on each side of the road and three in the center beside the jeep," he replied.

Agent Manning repositioned the lead car behind the Suburban so that the limo was the first vehicle to approach the roadblock. This was done in part so that military commanders could plainly see that this was the US ambassador and his bodyguards and, in part, so that we could implement any "crash and bang" measures with the limo, if necessary. If we did have to crash the jeep out of the way, we wouldn't want to involve the lead vehicle first because, if it got hung up, the limo would have little chance of getting through two vehicles.

Our motorcade cautiously approached the manned roadblock where I saw the officer, now only a few hundred feet in front of the limo, hold up his hand in a gesture for us to stop. We crept ever forward. He now put up both hands and used a police type whistle to get us to stop. As the limo approached him, I leaned toward the windshield and waved to him as we proceeded around the jeep. He had stepped out of the way, realizing that we weren't going to stop. When the limo got past the jeep, all hell broke loose! Gunfire erupted from both sides of the road as several men dressed in green, army-style uniforms began firing. Bullets were exploding; some were slamming into the sides of the limousine and follow car.

"GO! GO! GO!" I shouted into my radio microphone. "Get down, Mr. Ambassador!"

Agent Fox pressed the gas pedal to the floorboard. As we accelerated, I unbuckled my seatbelt and bolted from the front seat into the back, continuing to yell at Ambassador Devine. "Get down! Get down!" I threw myself on top of him. Now both of us were sprawled out on the back seat. Using my hand closest to the floor, I grabbed the Kevlar blanket and pulled it on top of us. The blanket was made of the same fabric used in bulletproof vests that agents wear under their shirts. I had my vest on so that if bullets penetrated the limo's armored body they would still have either gotten caught in the Kevlar or drilled into me instead of the ambassador. The two-way radio had been torn off my waist belt during the leap, and my earpiece, which had been attached to the radio, was dangling by its unattached cord from my ear. The thundering crash of more bullets echoed inside the vehicle. Each bullet was trying to burrow its way through the metal and into our bodies. But the vehicle's armor held. Seeing that the road ahead was clear, Fox floored the accelerator pedal and sped away from the attackers who were still firing at us from both sides of the road.

"Are they chasing us?" I yelled to Fox. What do you see? Turn up the volume on the car radio!"

Fox had slid down in the seat and was totally focused on speeding us away from harm. The three vehicles were each equipped with two-way car radios set to the same frequency as our portable radios. I heard Special Agent Bob Beam, the Shift leader, who was riding in the front seat of the Suburban call out,

"We're still taking hits. But we're right on your tail. Go! Go! Go!"

Fox continued burying the gas pedal into the floorboard of the limo. There was no opportunity for the agents to return fire. We had quickly sped beyond the range of the gun ports, which were mounted in the doors of the Suburban. All three vehicles continued speeding away. Seconds later we heard Bob on the radio. "We're clear of the roadblock." After about a minute, Agent Manning radioed from the Plymouth Fury, now the tail car. "They don't seem to be following, he reported. "They're staying behind! Oh, God! My foot! My foot! He shouted. It feels like it's on fire!"

"Beam to Manning, what's going on back there!" Beam surmised the Plymouth may have caught on fire from being hit by bullets. There was no response. Manning was still following a hundred feet behind the Suburban. Beam glanced at his side view mirror and over his shoulder, as did the other agents riding in the Suburban.

"Beam to Manning . . . Fred, there's no smoke! Are you OK?" "I think I've been shot!" Manning replied. "My foot's burning like hell!"

"Can you keep going, Fred?" Beam asked Manning, who was alone in the Plymouth.

"Yeah, I can."

I pushed myself off the ambassador and back into the front seat. I leaned over and helped the ambassador up. "Are you all right, Sir?" The words nervously spewed out of my mouth.

"Yes, Mr. Schenck, I believe I am," he answered with an almost totally calm voice. "I'm not quite sure what just happened. Are you OK?"

"I'm OK, Sir." I settled into my seat and grabbed the hand mic on the car radio. "OK, Fred . . . everyone's OK. Let's get to the embassy." The embassy was still about two miles away. Tom Fox was tearing up the road as he sped onward. Agent Beam came on the radio.

"Beam to base, we're ten clicks away."

"Roger that, Beam . . . we're ready," said a Marine. The radio base station located in the Marine's office at the Chancery was on the same frequency as the agents' radios. Chris and Gunny also had portable radios on the same frequency. They had heard everything. Since there were three entrances to the Chancery compound, we used numbers to identify to the Marine guards which entrance we had selected: 1, 2, 3.

Just as the detail had varied the routes and times each day, we also varied our points of entrance into the embassy. We would only call it out five minutes prior to arrival each day so that the Marine Security Guards could be standing by.

"Beam to base, five clicks away . . . Entrance 3 . . . I say again, Entrance 3."

Wisely, Agent Beam had chosen the underground garage entrance. "Roger that . . . Entrance 3," repeated the Marine Guard. As we arrived at the gate, we saw Chris, Gunny and several Marines standing in the street, all with automatic rifles poised and ready in case the bad guys were lurking behind the motorcade. The gates swung open quickly as the limo and Suburban follow car squealed into the compound. We sped on down the long drive-ramp and entered the garage. Agents jumped out of the Suburban and surrounded the limo.

"All clear," Beam announced by radio. I released the door locks, stepped out of the limo and opened the right rear door. Manning had halted the Plymouth inside the perimeter gate and was being helped out by Chris and Gunny. An embassy vehicle with driver was standing by to take him to the hospital. Still unable to emotionally release himself from duty, Manning radioed to me.

"Schenck, Manning . . . all clear?"

"We're all clear, Fred. You get to the hospital. We'll see you there soon. Great job, Fred."

Ambassador Devine emerged from the limo and stood in the garage with us as we began searching for and counting bullet markings. He seemed to be regaining his composure as were the rest of us regaining ours. There were multiple bullet indentations in the body of the Suburban and shattered cracks on the ballistic glass on the right side. We found eight more bullet indentations in the body of the limo. Not a single bullet had penetrated the armor of the vehicles. The bullet that did strike Manning had found its way through the unprotected, left front wheel well and through the dashboard of the Plymouth Fury sedan.

We could only conjecture why the attack happened. Ambassador Devine said he was going to make it his immediate priority to find out. He would be on the telephone to the Minister of Defense within minutes. Beam and I escorted him over to the staircase and climbed upward one floor to the waiting elevator. From there we escorted him to his third-floor office, then returned to the garage.

Later that day we received both good news and very disturbing news. The good news was that Fred was out of the hospital. He had returned to the Chancery on crutches, with his foot in a partial cast. The bullet had fractured his ankle but had bounced off the bone, but failing to lodge inside. He would be OK. The bad news was that a regular Salvadoran army unit had conducted the roadblock. Apparently, a young, overzealous lieutenant either hadn't gotten the order to let the US ambassador's motorcade pass through, or he had ignored it. There was some speculation by Ministry of Defense officials that the lieutenant was out to make a name for himself among his troops, to show them that no one could defy his orders. As we escorted the ambassador to his residence that evening, he quipped,

"I imagine right about now that lieutenant is probably hanging by his thumbs from some dark, damp jail cell, Mr. Schenck. I've received no less than a dozen calls today, as has Colonel West, from high-ranking military and government officials expressing their profound apologies and implying as much."

"Really!" I exclaimed. "Well, Sir, as if we don't have enough bad guys to contend with, now we know for sure we can't even trust the good guys!"

"Who said the Salvadoran military are the good guys?" the ambassador retorted.

His comment told such a large part of the real story in El Salvador. "Point well taken," I said. "It's getting worse with less order and obedience by the troops each day, isn't it Sir?"

"I'm afraid so, Steve," he replied almost philosophically. "The government and military are breaking down. It's not at all good, not at all."

As the limo turned through the opened gate of the Ambassador's Residence, Devine said, "Well, you've managed to provide me with another extraordinary day, Mr. Schenck. My wife's not going to believe this one!"

In the year that I had been protecting him, our motorcade had never encountered an attack. We attributed this, in part, to the diverse routes planning and the varied times of our departures and arrivals. This day had been our first brush with near disaster. The limo came to a halt at the pillared front-porch. I stepped out and opened the door. As the ambassador exited, he held out his hand to shake mine.

"Thank you, Steve, for all that you and your guys did today. Please tell everyone how much I appreciate it."

"I will, Mr. Ambassador." With that said, I bid him good night and watched as a very tired man turned to walk into his home. His usually perfectly pressed suit was badly wrinkled. His normally professionally erect stature now slumped. He looked worn out. For more than three years Ambassador Devine had faced serious threats and had read many Intelligence reports warning him that that Leftist Guerillas would try to end his life. Yet, in spite of it all, he had chosen to boldly ignore the perils facing him. The ambassador was not to be dissuaded from his effort at bringing peace to El Salvador and better living conditions for its people. But it was clear to me that El Salvador was taking its toll on this eagle of diplomacy.

In early March, 1980, with his tour of duty as ambassador to El Salvador completed, Frank J. Devine and his wife Barbara were being escorted on a final ride in the black, armored Cadillac. Ahead of them was a twenty-five-mile journey on the highway to the international airport, a highway well known for its dangers to motorists, terrorist roadblocks, kidnappings, and gun shots fired randomly at vehicles. As usual, I was riding in the right front seat. Fred Manning, having recovered from his bullet wound, was again driving the Plymouth Fury lead car. The remaining DS agents of this remarkably brave detail of civilian soldiers were riding in the armored Suburban follow-up car. Frank Devine comforted his wife by holding her hand. Both of them realized all that they had survived during the time they had been in El Salvador. All was very quiet inside the limousine, save for an occasional remark about the distance to the airport. The ambassador had traveled the road many times and kept his own mental set of mile markers. He said to his wife,

"Five miles down, dear, and only twenty to go," and a few minutes later, "ten miles gone and only fifteen to go," and so on. We arrived at El Salvador's international airport where Chris was waiting. He had gone out to the airport earlier and made special arrangements so we could avoid the crowds and immigration officials. We drove around to a side entrance and escorted Ambassador and Mrs. Devine into the same VIP lounge where they had been welcomed upon their arrival in October of 1977. After a few minutes wait, we heard the announcement for boarding of the Pam American flight to Miami. We exchanged final farewells, and Chris and I walked with them onto the aircraft. Once they were comfortably seated in First Class, we bid them a final good-bye handshake and exited the aircraft. Chris, the other agents, and I all remained in the VIP Lounge for the next twenty minutes, when, at last, the airplane was wheels up. A profound sense of relief came over me as we exchanged glances and shook each other's hands. Relief turned into jubilation at the realization that we had kept the ambassador out of harm's way and that we lived to tell about it. Our mission to protect one of the two most threatened US ambassadors in the world was a success. In early March 1980, Ambassador Devine said goodbye to diplomacy and retired from the Foreign Service. He returned to his home in Washington, D.C., battle fatigued and weary. In 1981 he published his memoirs, a fascinating and detailed account of his tenure as US ambassador in a book entitled *El Salvador: Embassy under Attack.* Therein, he gave credit to his team of DS Special Agents, recounting some of the sobering experiences we shared together.

What we had all endured in succeeding in the mission of protecting Ambassador Devine and the embassy had emptied us in body and mind. Yet, there would be little rest. One week later we were back at the airport awaiting the arrival of Robert E. White, the next ambassador to El Salvador. Our mission would begin all over again.

White had been on the job one week when, on March 24, 1980, Ambassador Devine's friend and outspoken champion for the masses of the poor in El Salvador, Archbishop Oscar Romero was assassinated. Ninety percent of El Salvador's population is Catholic. If there was any doubt as to the lengths extremists in El Salvador would go, it was proven beyond a doubt that fateful day. He was gunned down during mass in the afternoon. This event marked only the second time in world history that a Catholic Archbishop had been slain. This tragedy was cause for great concern for us and was shocking to the entire diplomatic corps in El Salvador and in Washington. Since a terrorist organization was willing to commit an unthinkable act such as this, so devastating to the Salvadorans who loved him, they would not hesitate to try and kill a US ambassador or other diplomat.

CHAPTER 19

BY SPECIAL ORDER OF THE PRESIDENT

The Fatal Crib

March 24, 1980.

"Things are growing much worse in El Salvador," President Carter began at a private meeting in the Oval Office. "Our influence with the governing junta in El Salvador has weakened considerably, and there are signs that the government is deteriorating rapidly. Moreover, the assassination of Archbishop Romero has spiraled the country into chaos. There is danger everywhere, especially for American citizens and our embassy personnel. Would you agree, Mr. Secretary?"

"Yes, Mr. President, I must agree. The situation is worsening daily, and Americans are in grave danger."

Carter was speaking to his Secretary of State, Cyrus Vance. "Cyrus, we already have one major hostage situation on our hands (US Embassy in Teheran) and I don't want to risk another. The country couldn't stand a second takeover of a US embassy and kidnapping of American diplomats. How is the downsizing going?"

"Mr. President, some of the embassy personnel and families have already left. The new ambassador--Robert White--is in place."

Carter spoke. "We must expedite the downscaling of embassy personnel. I want all non-essential US diplomats and all spouses and children to leave immediately. Put a 'No Travel' restriction into effect to keep others (US citizens) from going there. Do you agree?"

"Yes, I do," said Vance. "We will start immediately."

In unison, the other attendees present gave a resounding, "Thank you, Mr. President."

Representatives from the CIA, military Intelligence, and two other high ranking State Department officials in charge of Latin American affairs, had all been part of this meeting which ultimately set the stage for a life-altering experience for those of us at the US Embassy in El Salvador.

A summary of the March 24, 1980 meeting concerning El Salvador that was held by President Carter and Secretary of State Vance was shared by secured telegram with Ambassador Robert White. White first shared the telegram's contents with embassy senior officers and me. The telegram from the Secretary had instructed White to expedite the downsizing. The instructions were clear: get the non-essential, diplomatic personnel and all of the spouses and families in motion and out of the country with the utmost of haste. Begin on March 25, 1980.

On March 25, 1980, Ambassador White gave a summary of the decision that had been made in the Oval Office to the Embassy Diplomats and local staff. Of the more than one hundred fifty

American diplomatic personnel who, along with their families were in San Salvador, only forty diplomats and some local staff would remain. Chris Disney and I were designated as part of the contingent of those who would stay.

Here is a recap regarding the fateful rescue attempt of the 52 American hostages captured and held in Iran for 444 days, in 1979 and 1980. The 2012 movie *Argo* (Warner Bros. and GL Films Inc.), starring Ben Affleck, was based on the hostage crisis. In November of 1979, the US embassy in Iran was stormed by about three thousand hostile Iranian student-demonstrators. Americans were captured and taken hostage. Actually, the seizure was led by the Iranian Revolutionary Guard, a state-sponsored terrorist regiment directed by the Khomeini regime. Four months later, in February 1980, the Americans were still held in captivity. Carter feared for their lives and didn't want another embassy hostage situation. Embassy personnel had already been downsized for several weeks. Assignments were curtailed early, and Foreign Services officers, along with their families, were assigned to other posts. The purpose of the downsizing was so that there would be fewer diplomats in the country and, therefore, fewer targets for the terrorists.

The Iranian hostage situation lasted 444 days from 11/04/1979 until 01/20/1981. It had caused Carter the greatest political debacle of his presidency and contributed greatly to his failure to be re-elected. Fifty-two American diplomats and administrative staff were taken hostage by fanatics loyal to the Ayatollah Khomeini. Some were tortured. All were badly mistreated and poorly fed. Carter couldn't negotiate their release. Finally, in April 1980, after months of unsuccessful peaceful negotiations, Carter and the National Security Council authorized a covert military rescue operation to free the hostages. The mission deployed the US Army's elite hostage unit—Delta Force—and support troops. Code-named "Eagle Claw," the rescue plan deployed six transport planes departing from Oman. Their destination was Desert One, a dirt road that would be used as an airstrip about two hundred miles southeast of Teheran. A squadron of 132 Delta Force troops was to act as the rescue unit to free the hostages. Nicknamed "Charlie's Angels" after Colonel Charles Beckwith, commander and founder of the unit, this elite team boarded the transport planes. They were to rendezvous with eight Marine Sea Stallion helicopters at Desert One, which were to fly in from the carrier *Nimitz* anchored in the Gulf of Oman. The squadron, concealed in trucks, would enter the city, assault the embassy compound at night, overpower the guards and, in the end, take the hostages to a soccer stadium where they would board helicopters and eventually ride out of Iran.

The transports reached their destination and secured the site. However, the helicopters had trouble right from the start, running headlong into a sandstorm. Consequently, the helicopters developed either mechanical or instrumentation problems, forcing them to abandon their ships or return to the *Nimitz.* Only six of the eight aircraft ever made it to Desert One, way short of the required number of helicopters and men needed for the planned rescue. The operation was far behind schedule, suffering from the chaos and short of sufficient troops to ensure a successful mission. A daring plan had gone wrong. Within just a precious few hours the operation ended in disaster in the barren Iranian desert, with the loss of five airmen and three marines. (This Delta Force account is based on *Terrorism's War with America: A History,* by Dennis Piszkiewicz.)

As soon as the news of the attempted but failed rescue reached us, the two special operations soldiers got on the phone to their colleagues, in Delta Force, some of whom had participated in the mission. I got a first-hand account from them as to why the mission had failed. Both of them mumbled obscenities about the "goddamned politician generals." Apparently, there had been disagreement among the Joint Chiefs as to which of the military's helicopters would be used in the mission. Each member wanted his branch to play a role in the rescue. The Army had Delta Force, but the Air Force was to actually fly Delta Force and their equipment to the remote Iranian desert site in transport planes. Meanwhile, the Navy insisted that their helicopters be used to fly the hostages out of Iran. In the sandstorm one of the pilots became disoriented and flew in the wrong direction, eventually returning to the carrier 200 miles away. Rotor blade trouble forced another copter to crash in the desert, killing the two pilots. Then, after landing at the staging area, crews found that failed hydraulic boosters crippled a third helicopter. These helicopters were not adequately equipped for desert conditions, a crucial fact overlooked during the planning of the operation. Helicopters that were kept around water, especially salt water, for example, were outfitted differently than those used in dirt and sand conditions. To make matters worse, the aircraft had not been well-maintained due to lack of use and available parts.

Carter left office in January, 1981, with the Iranian crisis still unsettled. On January 20, 1981, President Reagan successfully gained freedom for the hostages. Two colleagues of mine, men who were Regional Security Officers at the embassy in Teheran-Alan Golisinski and Michael Holland--were among the hostages. Because they were regarded by their captors as CIA spies, they were severely mistreated. After being reunited with their families and recovery from their mistreatment, Allan returned to active duty, but Michael quietly left Diplomatic Security and the State Department. Allan chose to teach a special seminar offered by the Diplomatic Security Service to Foreign Service officers who were being assigned to foreign posts. The seminar was about how to survive as a hostage.

As stated earlier, my wife Janet had accompanied me to El Salvador in June, 1979. We had been married ten years but did not have any children. By early February of 1980, we had begun the process of adopting an infant Salvadoran child. The two-day-old infant had been placed in our home by a local adoption agency in

San Salvador, and we had been granted temporary custodial rights. According to law, an eight-week waiting period was mandated after we placed notice in the local newspaper of the intent to adopt the infant. We hired an attorney who prepared for the legal adoption through the local courts. Janet and I had named the infant Adam Carlos Schenck. We were in our seventh week of waiting when Ambassador White broke the news of the planned evacuation of dependents. So, the President's order had especially shocked and alarmed us. It meant that Janet would have to leave without our having completed the adoption! The balance of my tour in El Salvador would be spent on my own. What was to have been a two-year or more tour in El Salvador--with my wife and now my first child--abruptly ended after nine months.   San Salvador had fallen into chaos, with thousands of Salvadorans taking to the streets to bemoan his death of Archbishop Romero. Violent demonstrations broke out, directed angrily at the government and the military the demonstrators blamed for the assassination. The evacuation order US embassy called for a 24-hour time period to get all non-essential American diplomats and families out of the country. We were told that the dependents should pack for a week, since they would be going by an escorted convoy to the airport, then by plane to Guatemala City, in neighboring Guatemala. The idea was that at least *they* would be out of harm's way until the aftermath of the Romero assassination had settled down. Janet protested, as did some of the other wives. She called the ambassador late in the evening at his home.

"Mr. Ambassador, the adoption of our son is not complete. I have a job as a teacher at the American School. We're at the end of a marking period and I have grades to get out. I just can't leave!"

The ambassador replied, "I'm sorry, Mrs. Schenck, those grades won't matter if you are dead." We'll arrange for the Guatemalan Consulate here to give an emergency visa for the baby so he can travel with you. But you have to leave with the others."

Tight-lipped, Jan reluctantly thanked the ambassador and then hung up the phone. But her fury exploded seconds thereafter. She did not want to go!

"How can they make me go?" she sobbed. Shouting her tear-filled words, she kept on. "I'm independently employed as a teacher at the American School, and my employer is not telling me to leave!"

"But you are here as a dependent of a diplomat," I pleaded. "You're here under a diplomatic visa, not under a work visa. We have no choice."

We didn't sleep that night. In the morning Janet packed, overcome with anger. Janet and I amicably divorced in 1990 but have remained friends. In preparation for writing this book I called Janet and asked her if she could think about how she felt at the time she was being forced to leave El Salvador. When recalling the experience, Janet said,

"It was as if I was being gently pushed along by a great force on that day. I didn't feel I was doing any of the preparation for leaving. I don't remember physically packing and readying the baby or me for the trip. I didn't feel in control of my body or mind again until we were on our way to the airport."

In fact, I had driven her and the baby to the embassy, arriving at 5:45 a.m. on Monday, March 25th. The convoy, consisting of embassy vans and SUVs, some of which were armored, was lined up ready to accept its disgruntled passengers. Twelve heavily armed US Marines accompanied the convoy for protective escort. Those of us who remained to defend the ambassador, the embassy and its personnel bid our wives and children goodbye for what we thought would be one week. The plan called for their return in the last week of March, for a stay of duty we thought would be several more weeks before having to leave permanently.

The convoy left for the airport. The other agents and I went to our office and listened as the Marines communicated the convoy's progress by radio. Due to the death of Romero and the chaos that followed, the guard contingent was immediately doubled at the Chancery and at the Ambassador's Residence. Everyone was on duty that day. I prayed there wouldn't be a terrorist blockade set up on the road to the airport. Even with the well-armed Marines along, a hit on the convoy would surely bring about the casualties and deaths of our spouses and children. The hour-long journey to the airport seemed like an eternity for those of us who waited for word of their safe arrival. Finally, the Marines radioed news that the convoy had arrived at the airport without incident. Many hours later I was able to talk to Janet by phone as she and the baby, Adam, were resting comfortably in a hotel room in Guatemala.

Violence flared full-blown in the aftermath of the death of Archbishop Romero, with heavy fighting and casualties occurring on both sides. There were kidnappings and murders. By March 30th, those of us whose loved ones were now safely in Guatemala were given some bad news. The planned one week's stay in Guatemala was officially revised to a permanent departure. The White House had either changed its mind or had planned all along for the dependents not to return to El Salvador. Those of us ordered to stay were told that our dependents would be provided with a housing allowance so they could rent housing in the states for the remainder of our tour in El Salvador. They could select a US location of their choice. Many chose to be settled close to their parents or other families back in the States. However, Janet and I still had to finalize the legal adoption proceedings for Adam. Our Salvadoran attorney had scheduled the court hearing in San Salvador to be held the day after the mandatory, eight-week waiting period was to expire April 1, 1980.

Adam had only an emergency visa to Guatemala. It became imperative that I seek a solution with the help of Ambassador White.   I was rolling through the streets of the city with the ambassador in the limousine, an Uzi cradled in my lap. A car full of gun-toting Special Agents escorted us in the follow-up vehicle behind. Because I accompanied the ambassador in the limousine daily, I had more opportunity to speak with him than even his highest of chief assistants. Although I seldom took such liberty, I decided to take it now.

"Mr. Ambassador?" I began hesitantly.

"Yes, Steve." Ambassador White, though only in the country for a few weeks, had the enviable ability to recall personal details and names of almost any of his staff's family members and situations. He knew many of their personal circumstances, whether someone had a special need going on in their household, difficult problems, or illnesses. His caring and compassionate nature doubtless helped him in foreign policy negotiations. I assumed he already knew what I was about to discuss.

"Sir, you're aware of the adoption process my wife and I are involved in."

"Of course," he replied. "How is it coming along?"

I explained our dilemma to him. Then he addressed me calmly and with a caring sound to his voice:

"Steve, I understand your problem. I really hope there is something that can be worked out. But my orders at present are very clear and come from the top. There is no room for exceptions in these orders. Our deadline for all dependents to be out of El Salvador is March 31st. We'll look into your problem in greater detail over the next few days. But at present I can't be more optimistic, I'm sorry to say."

I called Janet every night that week. After several long nights, I still had no good news to share with her. Things began to look dire. Then, while driving the ambassador home one Friday evening, he unexpectedly shared a telegram he had received earlier in the day from the office of the Secretary of State. It read,

"By special permission from the Secretary of State, Janet Schenck is given a 24-hour reprieve to return to El Salvador. By orders of the President of the United States she will be allowed to complete the adoption process, finish her business at the American School, and then immediately and permanently leave the country."

And so it was that on Tuesday, April 1, 1980, at 8:00 a.m., I met Janet and the baby at El Salvador's International Airport, where they had arrived from Guatemala City. On the way back to San Salvador she explained that many of the other dependents were rooting for us and had wished her and the baby farewell. We drove to the courthouse in San Salvador where Adam Carlos Schenck was pronounced legally ours. Then we drove to the embassy and obtained a visa so Janet could bring Adam into the United States. That afternoon she returned to complete her duties at the American School while I stayed home with the baby. I don't think I let him out of my arms that entire afternoon. We cradled together in a hammock near the pool while the cool breeze of the day rocked us gently. I know I sang quietly to him and told him how much I loved him. He was only eight-weeks old but I thought he had smiled up at me several times that afternoon. He seemed as contented and happy as I was.

First-time fatherhood is something I never thought I would experience. It awakened a feeling in me that was so different and emotionally bonding that it made the career I had chosen, achieved, and was mesmerized by, seem now more like just an ordinary job. Before Adam had arrived, I couldn't wait for the next day to come and to see the adventure that was to unfold. After Adam's birth, I yearned to stay home as long as possible and to return home from my job at the embassy as soon as possible. Of course, none of that was to be.

Janet returned home from a final day at school where she had completed her work and bid farewells to the other teachers and staff.

"Where's Adam?" Janet wanted to see the baby and hold him. "In his crib . . . we've had a wonderfully quiet afternoon. I think we've really bonded," I joked. We had placed the crib in a foyer, which was in the center of the second floor, adjoined by the three bedrooms and a bath. It was positioned just outside the doorway to our bedroom. She went upstairs, and I followed her. She held Adam in her arms and rocked him while I packed for the next morning's flight to the States.

On Wednesday morning April 2nd, a driver from the embassy pulled up in front of the house. He was driving one of the armored

SUVs. We were driven to the national airport where we caught a plane to Miami International. We then boarded a second flight to Grand Rapids, Michigan, touching down hours later at the Gerald R. Ford International Airport. A small greeting party comprised of our parents and several of our brothers, sisters, and their families, welcomed us home. It was a homecoming filled with mixed emotions. On the one hand, we were bringing home our first and only child for all to see. On the other hand, our return marked the beginning of a few fleeting days I would get to spend with my wife and new baby before returning to ever increasingly dangerous duty in El Salvador. The new experience of fatherhood was to last for the one week's leave I was given to personally take Janet and Adam to Grandville, Michigan, where they would start looking for a place to settle. Both our families lived close by, and we had good friends there, especially Larry and Karen Tuttle, who made room for Janet and Adam in their home for some months until Janet found a house to rent.

The night of our arrival, we gathered with my parents in their living room, enjoying the reunion. About 11:00 p.m. the phone rang. My mother took the call in the kitchen. She peered around the corner into the living room and said,

"Steve, it's the embassy calling. Your boss, Chris, is on the phone." Everyone stopped talking as I got up to answer the call.

"Hi, Chris."

"Steve," he said in a light and cheerful voice, "Did you make it home all right?"

"Yes, everything's fine. Everyone's fussing over the baby. I know you know what it's like, Chris, having two boys of your own."

"I sure do. Steve, I'm extremely happy that things worked out so well for you and your wife. You can truly say that your son received the blessing of the president of the United States! Not too many people can say that about one of their children!"   "You're so right, Chris. We feel really privileged."   "Well, I'm calling because you need to know what has happened down here, and Janet needs to know, too, so that it may comfort her a little. I know how disappointed and upset she was to have to leave El Salvador. Steve, I have some unfortunate news." Chris's voice became very sober and quivered a little. "Tonight around 9 o'clock someone planted a bomb across the street from your home. It exploded, and the damage to your home is extensive. It blew out all of the window glass."

My mind immediately envisioned the location of Adam's crib. Two large jalousie glass windows, each 4 feet by 16 feet, were close to Adam's crib. They extended the entire length of the two floors and were on the front house wall facing the street. Chris continued:

"I've returned from inspecting the house. We've put guards there until the landlord can get the windows boarded up. Steve, there's glass everywhere! I went upstairs. The force of the blast shot shards of glass, which pierced the baby's crib and mattress. Had Adam been in that crib when the bomb exploded, I don't think he would have survived. But I don't want you to worry. I'll make sure everything is secured. We'll begin an immediate investigation to see if it was your home that was specifically targeted or one of your neighbor's. Call me in a couple of days and I'll have an update for you. In the meantime, I know now that the right decision was made. It's gotten too dangerous down here for our wives and children."

"Thanks, Chris, thanks a lot. I really appreciate what you're doing down there for me. Talk with you soon."

When I soberly told Janet and the rest of the family the news, we all came to the same conclusion. God was watching over us. The feeling that Janet had felt earlier about being pushed along she now came to believe was the Almighty's guiding hand. Adam almost certainly would have been in his crib that night when the bomb exploded. If we had not left earlier that day, he would have been severely injured or killed. Had Adam been killed, we would have died too, perhaps not physically but emotionally just the same.

Two days later, Chris informed me by phone that our home was not, in fact, the target of the bombing. It was, instead, a wealthy Salvadoran businessman who lived across the street. Apparently, an assassin had placed a satchel filled with explosives up against the businessman's steel garage door. The poorly placed explosives sent a violent shock wave across the street, blowing out the windows in our house. Ironically, the blast did little damage to the home of the intended victim.

CHAPTER 20

THE KIDNAPPING OF EDUARDO GUERILLO

Kidnappings had become a constant threat. They consumed much of Chris' and my time. But since we were without families, we worked many sixteen-hour days. Chris was responsible for assisting US corporations and American family members in El Salvador in the event of a kidnapping. But as more and more kidnappings mounted, he assigned some of the responsibility to me. I thereby assumed the role of the US government's liaison officer working alongside hostage rescue teams. Outside experts were usually brought in to negotiate with the terrorist organization demanding the ransom. US corporations that operated in Central and Latin America in the 1970s carried high-premium insurance policies to help pay stiff ransoms if one of their employees was taken hostage. In a hostage rescue effort of a kidnapped US business leader the corporation most often hires a private hostage negotiator. The negotiator is usually from a security firm that specializes in protection and hostage negotiation. The 2000 movie, *Proof of Life,* starring Russell Crowe and Meg Ryan, gives an accurate portrayal of what a real-life negotiator encounters.

In April of 1980 I was intimately involved in a kidnapping rescue mission to gain the release of a wealthy Salvadoran, Eduardo Guerillo. Eduardo's wife Wendy was an American citizen. She was an acquaintance of mine who had come specifically to me to ask for help. Since Eduardo was not an American citizen, I explained to her that there was nothing the embassy could officially do. However, I discussed the matter with Ambassador Robert White and told him that I would like to do whatever I could to help her. He said,

"Keep it unofficial; never speak as if you're stating an official US government position in the matter. Then do what you can."   I thanked him, cleared it with Chris, and called Wendy to tell her I'd be working on the case. She was exuberant.

Wendy Guerillo was an American from a well-to-do Bostonian family. Several months before the kidnapping, I had come to know her and Eduardo at various functions that were attended by embassy personnel, along with American and Salvadoran civilians for social exchange. I had also once been invited to one of the Guerillo family's cotton plantations where Wendy and Eduardo graciously entertained several diplomats and me. The plantation was just one of several magnificent properties owned by Eduardo and his family.

Wendy was an extremely attractive, thirty-two-year-old woman who looked very much like a young Maria Shriver (later Maria Shriver-Schwarzenegger). She and Eduardo had met ten years earlier at a college in the United States. They married, and she returned with Eduardo to El Salvador where she lived the life of an elite socialite. Meanwhile, Eduardo tended to the family business of growing cotton and coffee.

When Eduardo was kidnapped, Wendy felt she needed someone she knew and who she could trust. In her eyes I was that man. For three weeks I worked on a hostage task force seeking Eduardo's release. Eduardo's family had hired two hostage negotiators from a Miami-based security company—Ackerman and Polumbo. They assisted me and were very helpful. Their local sources sometimes had useful information about kidnappers or the condition of kidnapped victims. Eduardo's parents, brothers and sisters, and their families had fled to Miami a year earlier, fearing their own kidnappings, as did many other wealthy Salvadorans. Eduardo had remained in El Salvador in order to manage the family businesses.

The family tried to negotiate the $5 million ransom demand. Wendy was to be the go-between who would bring the money from Miami into El Salvador. I would provide her with protective escort from the airport to a safe house that we had arranged for her whenever she brought money into El Salvador. It was not safe for her to stay in her own house. In the course of three weeks Wendy flew to Miami four times. Each time she returned carrying a suitcase laden with hundreds of thousands of dollars in US currency. Only Chris Disney and I knew of Wendy's itinerary. After meeting her at the airport, I drove her to the safe house in San Salvador, a distance of about twenty-five miles. At that time there was only one paved road between San Salvador and the country's only commercial airport. Even though the road was closely patrolled by Salvadoran military, it was treacherous because elusive thieves and terrorists found ways of setting up roadblocks. On these perilous journeys, Wendy would drive a non-descript vehicle like an older Volkswagen while I sat in the front passenger's seat. She carried a .38 caliber, 6 shot handgun in her jacket pocket. I carried an Uzi submachine gun and my Browning semiautomatic pistol. Altogether, from the four trips to Miami, she brought a total of over $3 million cash. Each time we made the trip I prayed we wouldn't be stopped. We never were. Each time we returned with money we drove directly to the embassy where Wendy would turn the money over to the mediators who made the money drops at pre-negotiated locations. They had been warned by the terrorist negotiator never to linger after making a drop. Instead, the mediators were to leave the money in a mail pouch-like cloth bag at a pre-arranged location and then return to the embassy. After several drops, culminating in the $3 million in cash being handed to the terrorists, Eduardo's family told the negotiators that they didn't have any more money to give. They instructed the negotiators to get the terrorists to settle for $3 million of the $5million originally demanded. Upon hearing this, Wendy was livid. She knew that the family was capable of paying more. She called Eduardo's father in Miami and pleaded with him to change his mind.

"Please don't tell the negotiators that there is no more," she beseeched him. "Perhaps the terrorists will negotiate for less than $5 million, but we can't gamble with Eduardo's life by closing the door to further negotiations." Her pleadings did not change the old man's mind. Eduardo's father and brothers were adamantly opposed to spending any more money. They were also being pressured by other friends and wealthy Salvadoran landowners that to give in to all of the terrorists demands would put many more of the families' members at risk of kidnapping. Eduardo's father tried explaining his dilemma to Wendy, but her mind would not be changed.

On a Monday morning, the fourth week of Eduardo's captivity, Commandant Zapata, an ex-Salvadoran police official, who was the chief of the Salvadoran police that guarded the embassy's perimeter, came into my office. Zapata was well informed about many of the terrorist and criminal happenings in San Salvador. For many years he served with the La Policía Nacional (the National Police) and had many contacts still working within the system. He appeared before me now, looking somber. Zapata knew how much I wanted to see the safe return of Eduardo.

Rather than giving his usual English greeting of "Good Morning, Señor Steve," Zapata stood silent and solemn. He was standing as if at attention.

"How are you this morning, Commandante?" I said, knowing that something was not right.

"Señor Steve, I'm afraid I have some very bad news. I have just been informed that police have found the body of Señor Guerillo. His body was found, still tied, lying along a road near the city limits. He was shot in the back of the head."

"My God," I uttered in disbelief. "Over $3 million collected and they still killed him. The . . . the . . . bastards!" The words barely came out. I, too, was struck with emotion. "Thank you, Alfredo."

I got up from behind my desk and walked over to the commandant to shake his hand while placing my left hand on his shoulder. He was a good man, and I deeply appreciated his loyalty. After he left the office, I walked down to a nearby conference room where I knew Chris was having a meeting with the negotiators. I knocked on the door and walked in. The look on my face brought an immediate question from Chris.

"What's wrong, Steve? You seem troubled."

"They've killed Eduardo. Zapata just informed me that the police found his body on a city street this morning; he'd been shot in the back of the head."

For three weeks Chris and I, along with the two professionals from Ackerman had concentrated our skills, resources, and energy in preventing this very outcome. Suddenly, there was no further need for the meeting. The negotiators said they would make arrangements to return Eduardo's body to Miami and would immediately inform Eduardo's family.

"I'll inform Wendy," I said. "She's due to arrive at the embassy within the hour."

"Is there anything I can do, Steve? Do you want me with you when you see Wendy?"

"Thanks, Chris, but I can handle it. Would you please inform the ambassador?"

"I'll go and see him right now, Steve. Please tell Wendy how very sorry Phiona (Chris's wife) and I are . . . will you?"

"Of course, Chris." I thanked the two negotiators, bid them farewell, and solemnly walked to the main gate entrance to await Wendy's arrival.

I recall all too well meeting Wendy as she drove up and parked her car, for what she thought was to be another meeting with the negotiators. She stepped out of the car and turned to greet me. Upon seeing the grave look of sadness upon my face, she broke into unstoppable tears. I held her for several minutes until she could compose herself. I don't recall the words that we exchanged. All she could muster were sobs of grief.

Wendy agreed to let me drive her back to the safe house. I spent the rest of the day guarding and consoling her while she grieved. Throughout the entire kidnapping drama, she had been brave and optimistic. She had traveled thousands of air miles and had personally placed her life in grave danger numerous times while carrying the ransom money. All in all, she had gotten very little sleep. The news of her husband's death and the sheer exhaustion she had undergone had driven her into a state of near hysteria.   At the safe house one of Eduardo's brothers called. She would not speak with him, so I did. She wanted nothing to do with any of Eduardo's family. In her mind they had chosen money over her husband's life. She knew that they could have met the ransom demand. Her brother asked me to tell Wendy that he was making funeral arrangements and that they arranged to have Eduardo's body flown to Miami. I hung up the phone and conveyed the message. Wendy cried, cursed and sobbed for hours. She talked. I listened. At one point she said,

"Eduardo's father was determined never to pay the entire ransom amount. He was certain the kidnappers would take less. How could he be so stupid? Damn him! Damn all of them and their greed!"

By now, she had been drinking several mixed drinks of whiskey and Coke. The hour grew late. Wendy got up from the chair in which she had been sitting and walked over to me. I had been seated on a small couch across from her. She held out her hand so that I should stand. As I stood up, she embraced me tightly. I returned the embrace.

"Don't let go," she pleaded in tears. "Please Steve, stay with me tonight."

She rested her head on my shoulder, pulling me ever closer. She sobbed and pleaded softly in a whisper, "Don't let go . . . don't let go."

I held her tightly. I sensed that she was emotionally exhausted and very frightened.

"Of course, I'm going to stay with you," I said. I helped her into the bedroom and we lay down on the bed. I cradled her in my arms as she rested her head upon my shoulder. Moments later, she fell into a deep sleep. I pulled the blanket so as to cover her shoulders. Then I, too, drifted off.

We awoke the next morning at 7:00 a.m. She felt a little better, having had the first full night's sleep in some time. I made coffee, and we sat at a small table and spoke briefly.

"You have done more for me than anyone else. You have been so understanding and kind through all of this." Her voice trembled with emotion. She gently took my hand into hers and continued, saying,

"I want to go home . . . to Boston to be with my parents and sister."

"I'll do anything I can to help you, Wendy. Whenever you're ready to leave, I'll take you to the airport."

"Steve, I need to tell you something. But please, don't share this with anyone."

"What is it?" I asked, vowing to keep her secret.

"I wasn't in love with Eduardo. I loved the life I've had here, and I had everything money could buy. But he was always conducting business. I was alone so much of the time. He was seldom ever there for me. I had to be so strong, and so much of the time I felt like I was just his trophy piece." Her voice cracked with emotion.

"I didn't feel the love for him that I should have . . . as his wife." I sat beside her, holding her hand as she spoke. A minute or two later I said, "Wendy, I understand. But none of what we're enduring here in El Salvador is anything close to being normal. Each day, I think about returning to my family, especially now that I have a child. Hopefully, it will be better for you when you return to the states, reunite with those who love you, and begin to feel safe again. Don't dwell on the way this has ended. It's too horrible. Remember the good times and the once in a lifetime experience you had while living here."

"I'll try," she said. "I'll try." She called Pan American reservations and was able to reserve a seat on the flight to New York leaving at 12:15 p.m.

"Would you have time to drive me to the airport?" she asked in her ever-courteous manner. I readily agreed to do so. On the way there she talked about her future.

"I will stay with my parents and take some time to sort out my life," she vowed. "In due time, I'll have to return to El Salvador and close things out here. So, Steve, will I see you again?"   "I don't know, Wendy. It's crazy here and I have many demands on my time."

"Well, you must come to Boston some day and let me show you around. I want you to meet my parents and my sister, Claudia."

"I'd like that very much," I said. We arrived at the terminal and I delivered her bags to an awaiting attendant. At the gate we gave each other a final embrace. During this intense time, we had really come to care for one other. We now shared an immeasurable bond of trust and the feeling of having lived through a tragedy of immense proportion. With the multiple rides during the hostage negotiations--some at night--from the airport to the safe house, carrying large sums of money, we had disregarded our own possible deaths in trying to save another's life. The embrace lingered. It was difficult for either of us to part. Then came the final boarding call. At last, the time for Wendy's nightmare had come to an end. She would return to Boston to be with her parents. Eduardo's body had been flown to Miami where his family held the funeral. I presumed Wendy was in attendance, but I do not know for certain. As it turned out, I never saw Wendy again.

CHAPTER 21

HELD HOSTAGE

It was a bright, warm Saturday morning in May 1980. Ambassador Robert E. White was working in his office at the embassy. He had been at his new job less than six weeks. White was a hardworking, career diplomat, with twenty-five years of service in the State Department. He had served in several Latin American countries and was the US Ambassador to Paraguay in the late 1970s. Now, he had come to El Salvador as President Carter's emissary for the promotion of human rights and agrarian reform, at a time when the country was on the verge of civil war. The ambassador had confronted human rights abuses, violence, and even murder at his previous posts. What he and those of us who protected him were about to experience in El Salvador would change us all forever.

The usually busy embassy was particularly quiet today. It was a Saturday. The embassy's regular complement of personnel had been vigorously downsized by orders of President Carter, and the few of us who remained worked on Saturdays. Of the twenty-four Marine Security Guards, six were on duty this day, as were a few of the local Salvadoran maintenance and motor pool personnel. White had called me earlier at home to tell me he wanted to go to the embassy and work until noon. So, the other detail agents and I accommodated his request, spent the morning at the embassy, and were now waiting in the security office for the return trip. We busied ourselves by cleaning the tools of our trade--automatic weapons, shotguns, and pistols. Around 10:30 a.m. the phone rang at my desk.

"Steve, it's Mel," Dark Knight said.

"Good morning, Mel. Don't tell me you're working, too, on this beautiful Saturday morning."

"Well, I did have plans to go to the beach, but one of my informants has changed all that. I think your plans will have to change, too."

"What's up?" I asked.

"My sources tell me there's going to be a march on the embassy. Members of some of the organizations on the Right are planning a demonstration for around 1:00 p.m. I have very little other details except that it is supposed to be peaceful."

"How many demonstrators, Mel?"

"The numbers are sketchy at best, but one source thought about three hundred. Listen, I can't talk more now, but I'll call you if I get more information. Good luck!"

"OK, Mel, thanks." I notified the other agents of the news. They agreed to do an office sweep throughout the embassy to alert anyone else who might be working that morning.

Mel's call was typical of the Intelligence reporting I received while in El Salvador. Often the information was sketchy. Even more often, frequent reports of impending demonstrations or attacks on the motorcade never materialized. Not that I was complaining. Any day that such reports failed to materialize into anything was a good day! The analysts' reports kept us ever vigilant, especially when they contained information about possible attacks. Information regarding such attacks almost never named an exact time, place, or method, but only that an attack was being planned. Sometimes the information received by my covert colleagues from their sources informed us that rebels were planning to detonate a car bomb as the motorcade passed by a "rigged" parked car. As for dates and times, all I ever got was "sometime in the coming weeks or days." I often caught myself holding my breath in dire anticipation as the limo carrying the ambassador and me passed slowly by a line of parked vehicles. It was discomforting, to say the least, to have received an Intelligence report stating that one of the Leftist Revolutionary army groups - FARN, BPR, or FPL--was planning to detonate a car bomb in an effort to kill the American ambassador, and then for me to be driving him throughout the city every day. But that was part of the job. For this very reason we altered the routes and varied our times of departure daily. Some of our routes took us through less crowded parts of the city and out into the surrounding countryside.

Throughout the entire time I was in El Salvador (1978-81), our greatest defense against dangers, such as remotely detonated car bombs, or ambushes on the motorcade, was the element of surprise. Each day, the agents played a game to see who could devise the most clever and circuitous route. Two agents, competing against each other and using maps, each conceived their own devised route between the Residence and the Chancery. Then the rest of us voted on which of the routes we thought to be the best. Some of our cleverly designed routes took us several miles in a completely opposite direction to our intended destination before circling back. Both Ambassadors Devine and White soon gave up trying to figure out where we were going or when they might arrive at the destination. Eventually, each of them just settled in the back seat and busied themselves reading the newspapers.

I recall once, while riding with Ambassador Devine back in 1979, that he became a little impatient with the morning ride to the Chancery from the Residence. This particular trip was taking much longer than usual to get to the office. In one such instance he said,

"Mr. Schenck, I have absolutely no idea where we are. We left my house more than thirty minutes ago and we don't seem to be any closer to the embassy than when we left. (A direct route would have taken no more than twenty minutes.) In fact, I think we might be farther away."

"What makes you think that, Mr. Ambassador?" I said, trying my best to contain an impulse to chuckle out loud.

"Well, when we left, I was being chauffeured through my plush, stately neighborhood of beautiful homes and paved roads, and toward the high-rise hotels and shopping district of San Salvador, in the direction of the embassy."

He loved to elaborate with flowery words of expression. He continued, his voice rising as he became more demonstrative. "As I look out my window now, I see tall, dried-out grass and brown clay fields, Brahma bulls and . . . water buffaloes! Such rustic scenery leaves me to conclude that I'm not getting any closer to my office. That is, unless you've cleverly managed to conceal it in a stealth-like manner--something I wouldn't put past the capacity of my friends in the Diplomatic Security Service!"

"We'll be there soon, Mr. Ambassador. Just think of this as a Sunday drive through the country."

I could barely contain myself from laughing out loud. His description was humorous, but he may have been trying to send me a message about his need to get to work as soon as was possible. I did miss his calm, even temper and eloquence.

My mind flashed back to May 1980. We had received new and more exact Intelligence suggesting that a demonstration against the embassy was imminent. Two of the Special Agents, Nick Gaines and Tom Fox, went about the embassy alerting other personnel of the impending demonstration. Gaines had replaced Bob Beam as the Shift Leader just two weeks earlier. I went upstairs to inform Ambassador White.

The Ambassador's Office was part of a three-office suite on the third (top) floor. The Deputy Chief of Mission (DCM), Mark Dion, was sitting in one of the outside offices and separated from the ambassador's office by an empty secretary's office. I knocked on the ambassador's closed door.

Ambassador White ushered me into his office with a commanding tone, as if he had been irritated by the interruption. "Come in."

I had apparently disturbed him from his reading. "Oh, it's you, Steve. What can I do for you?"

"Mr. Ambassador, I've just received information that Rightists are mounting a demonstration which is to occur around 1:00 p.m. today, here at the Chancery. It's supposed to be peaceful, but one never knows."

"Well, that should be interesting," White said. He had a very dry sense of humor, which I came to appreciate. In the six weeks that I had been protecting him, I still couldn't figure out when he was joking.

"Shall we watch it from the rooftop?" he said wryly.   "Hey, Dion," White called out to his Deputy Chief of Mission in the neighboring office. "Get in here."

Mark Dion, a tall and lanky man, was another career diplomat, fourteen years younger than White. Dion strolled in. His brown hair was thin, and he was partially balding from the forehead. Mr. Dion was a very amiable guy with a pleasant smile. He usually wore pinstriped shirts and preferred light brown or tan colored suits to the ambassador's more semi-formal dark blue or gray pinstriped suits. On this day both Dion and the ambassador wore navy blue and white, pinstriped, long-sleeved shirts, khaki slacks, and burgundy leather loafers. They were so dressed alike that when Dion walked into the ambassador's office, I was tempted to make one of those jokes about how they must have called each other to coordinate their wardrobes before coming to work that day. Not knowing them any better than I did, I decided not to poke fun at my new boss, a man who could alter the course of one's upward spiraling career if he so desired.

"Yes, Chief," Dion responded.

"Mr. Schenck tells me there's going to be a demonstration by Rightists against the Chancery this afternoon. I'm trying to figure out where you and I should stand to watch. Perhaps one of us should prepare a speech!"

"I'll bring the popcorn," Dion said.

"Great," replied the ambassador. "I'll bring the beer," he said with a chuckle. We all laughed.

"So, Steve, what do you want to do?" White asked.

This was good. The new ambassador was asking me. Though accustomed to giving orders and leading, he knew that when it came to his personal protection, I was in charge. If he didn't like my decision, he could have disagreed until he and I reached a compromise. In this case, it was obvious.

"Sir, I think we better depart from here soon and return to your residence. I've already alerted Tony and Gunny."

Anthony J. (Tony) Walander was also new to the embassy, having replaced Chris Disney as the senior Regional Security Officer about the same time that Ambassador White arrived. I hated to see Chris go. We had been through much together. But for his sake, he needed some respite from it all. During more than two years of service as Senior RSO, he'd seen more action and lived through more danger than most RSOs would probably ever experience. Walander was fresh to his post here, though not without experience, having served in other posts with a high-threat level. He was single and in his early thirties, while Chris was a devoted family man in his forties, who had been away from his wife and two adolescent sons for nearly a year. I continued my discussion with Ambassador White.

"Tony and Gunny will be bringing Marines and taking up defensive positions at the embassy. The Marines will make certain that everyone is out of the building and that it will be locked down within the hour."

"All right then, Steve. Let's depart in half an hour," the ambassador said. "I'll collect some things here and work from home the rest of the weekend. Mark, why don't you come along and work with me at the house this afternoon? We'll have someone bring your car out to the residence after this all blows over." "Fine with me," Mark said.

"All right then," I interjected. "I'll come to get you at 11 o'clock, Mr. Ambassador. Thank you."

At precisely 11:00 a.m. I returned to the ambassador's office. The other agents had finished their walk through the embassy and were in the underground garage preparing the vehicles for departure. Ambassador White was ready to go. He was holding a brown, leather briefcase in his left hand, and a stack of newspapers were tucked under his right arm. Each day he read newspapers published in San Salvador, along with the *Miami Herald, Washington Post,* and *New York Times,* so as to stay well informed of US and international news. His full head of graying hair was neatly parted to the right. He stood 5'11" tall and was a trim 180 lb. His face was very tan, revealing the pensive facial lines of someone who had been preoccupied with the enormity of global implications for his decisions. He was the prominent actor for the State Department whose diplomatic judgments in high stakes political affairs had worldly consequences, some which could help to determine the fate of millions of lives . . . lives that hung in the balance of American foreign policy.

"Catching up on your reading, Mr. Ambassador?" I quipped. "Well, that was the plan, Mr. Schenck, until you interrupted it," he fired back in a grumbling tone. "Now I'll have to read it all at home."

The ambassador, the DCM, and I walked out of the offices to the awaiting elevator. On the way down, we stepped up our verbal repartee. "Don't blame me!" I jostled him in return. "I'm just the messenger. It was Mel who called with the news of the demonstration. It's his information that we're acting on here, Sir."

"So, he's the culprit. I wondered how you had come about this news. Why's he working today, anyway?" White carried on in a humorous bent.

"Beats me, Sir, but I'm kind of glad that he is." The elevator arrived at the first floor. We walked around the corner and descended the flight of stairs to the garage. Once there, we entered the awaiting limo. Agent Gaines was standing at the open, right rear door of the black Cadillac. Agent Tom Fox was seated behind the steering wheel and had the motor running. Two other agents had surrounded the limousine, one with an Uzi machine gun in hand, the other carrying an automatic rifle. The twelve foot high, twenty-foot-wide steel door that secured the underground garage rolled open. The concrete drive ramp stretched a distance of 200 feet from the garage to the east gate of the embassy. Agent Fred Manning was in his usual position as driver of the lead car. His wounded foot was healing well, but he still walked with a slight limp. Fred was waiting outside the closed service entrance gate. The Fury was parked, with motor running, in the driveway apron perpendicular to the street. Manning's eyes darted sharply in all directions looking for any sign of trouble. Meanwhile, two Marines stood guard at the gate and controlled its movement. Minutes before, the agents had chosen one of the many circuitous routes we had carefully devised. After the rest of the motorcade caught up to

Manning, he finally turned the lead car onto the street. Any enemy plot to attack the motorcade after it left the embassy would have to include two different scenarios: one, if we had turned right out of the driveway, and second, if we had turned left. From inside the parked limo, I spoke into my sleeve microphone.

"Schenck to Manning . . . all clear?" The ambassador was seated behind me, and Mr. Dion was behind the driver.

"All clear," he replied.

"Let's go," I commanded. At the command, the agents retreated into the Suburban following close behind. As the limo and follow vehicle approached the perimeter gate, the two Marines opened the gate and stepped out into the street, their rifles ready, if necessary. On this day we turned right.

The trip to the Ambassador's Residence occurred without an incident, arriving at noon. Ambassador White and DCM Dion went inside. Except for Fox, who had to be elsewhere, I did not dismiss the detail. Though the ambassador said he'd be remaining home for the rest of the weekend, I felt it wise for us to remain with him awhile, since the Chancery, though a fair distance away, was being targeted for a demonstration. Two Marines were guarding the residence that day. At 1:15 p.m. I received a radio transmission to stand by the Marine guard post for a phone call. I walked over to the guard station inside the garage of the residence. The phone rang.

"Corporal Chavez," the Marine on duty answered. "Yes, Sir, he's right here." He handed me the receiver.

"This is Schenck." It was the Defense Attaché, Colonel West on the other end of the line. He was the embassy's military expert and chief US liaison with the Salvadoran military.

"Steve, it's Jerry. We've received information that there's going to be a large group of demonstrators marching in masse to the Ambassador's Residence. They're forming right now, about a mile away. We figure they'll be there in about 45 minutes-around 2 o'clock."

This information totally contradicted the CIA agent's earlier report.

"Are you sure?" I questioned. "I've received a conflicting report that—" but before I could finish my sentence Jerry interrupted.

"—I know, Steve. Mel and I have been communicating with one another. He's got his sources on the street. My information came from the Minister of Defense who called me about thirty minutes ago. But he doesn't want to order military intervention so long as the demonstrators are peaceful. He told me his officers would keep their eyes on things. You guys should be OK over there."

Easy enough for him to say, I thought. He wasn't here. Now, I had to ponder two completely different reports.

"OK, Jerry, thanks . . . I guess. Let me know if you get any clarification."

"No doubt about that," West replied. I entered the residence and informed Ambassador White of the situation. He and Dion conferred a minute about what to do, but they decided to remain at the residence.

The official embassy residence was a stately home on a street located in an upper-class area of the city. Palm trees and lush, brightly colored, flowered, tropical plants lined the street. Several other countries' ambassadors lived in this neighborhood. The neighbors were an interesting mixture of some of El Salvador's rich business owners, government officials, and foreign diplomats. National guardsmen and San Salvador's police force routinely patrolled the area. Most of the homes were enclosed with high-security fencing or concrete walls, most often painted white. Three years earlier, when Ambassador Devine first moved to the residence, elaborate security measures had been put into place. DS technicians came from headquarters in Washington to install high-tech security devices. They had mounted remote-controlled surveillance cameras with infrared (night vision) capability. Cameras covered the entire home: front, side, and backyards. We usually posted two Marines to guard the residence. One Marine patrolled the interior perimeter of the compound, while the other kept a constant visual on him with the aid of the remote-controlled cameras. The Marine post in the garage contained several monitors. Each monitor was connected to a different camera so that all cameras could be viewed simultaneously. Motion detection devices were positioned on the perimeter walls and along the grounds. If tripped, they triggered an audible alarm and activated a set of floodlights.

The backyard of the residence was approximately 100 feet wide by 150 feet long. There was a full-length swimming pool in the middle of the backyard. It was framed by a six-foot wide concrete walkway. A cabaña, brightly painted in sunny yellow with sky blue trim and furnished with a changing area, was erected on one side of the pool. White lattice encircled the small building, upon which crawled lush green vines and beautiful red and yellow roses. Several fruit-bearing trees and brightly colored, flowered bushes adorned the yard.

The front yard area of the home consisted mostly of the concrete circular drive, with a ring of grass growing in its center. A white flagpole stood in the center of the grass. It waved the Stars and Stripes 24/7. The flag was illuminated at night by a floodlight shining upward from the base of the pole. The circular drive made it convenient for chauffeured-driven vehicles to enter onto the property and pull up to the pillared porch to allow passengers to disembark. The driveway was big enough for about four vehicles. A twelve-foot high, white concrete wall secured the entire perimeter of the property. Sharp pieces of glass were embedded in the cement on top of the wall, and three parallel strands of barbed wire reinforced the glass. A large, black, sliding steel gate secured the driveway entrance from the street.

It was now 2:00 p.m. Ambassador White and DCM Dion remained inside. Four DS agents, two Marines, and I took up various strategic vantage points around the perimeter and inside the residence. I was positioned on the second floor where I had a view of the front-yard and driveway. Shortly after 2:00 p.m. RSO Tony Walander radioed that he was approaching the gate. He arrived with Gunny Saebo and two more MSGs. Colonel West had already alerted them. Walander said that there hadn't been any activity at the Chancery . . .yet. Just the same, he and Gunny left a dozen Marines there. With our augmented force, we established more defensive positions and waited for the demonstration to begin.

By 2:30, pick-up trucks, small and large sedans started to arrive. They parked on the street, in front of the residence. Protesters exited the vehicles and began gathering in the street in front of the residence. From my second-story position I could hear the chanting of hundreds of marching demonstrators coming from down the street. It sounded like they were about a block away, but my view of the street was partially obstructed by a high wall. So, we could only make out that portion of the street in front of the residence with the aid of a camera mounted on a corner of the wall. The size of the crowd grew to well over 200 by 3:30 p.m. Marchers had come from their staging area and were chanting and carrying signs. One of the demonstrators with a bullhorn in hand started shouting protests against US presence in El Salvador. The demonstrators did not appear to be from the Left. Though dressed in casual clothing they did not look ragged or poor. Many had arrived in their own vehicles. Their signs and banners proclaimed Ambassador White to be a Communist and that US policy was not wanted. Suddenly, the loud blare of a truck's horn and the rumbling of a diesel engine pierced the air. I could see puffs of black smoke rising upward from a truck that was moving slowly toward us. The protestors had driven a large flatbed truck to the scene. Two giant speakers and a microphone stand were mounted on its bed. As soon as the truck was parked on the far side of the street, about twenty protestors who were standing on the truck began broadcasting threats and obscenities. We spotted some protestors to be carrying rifles and pistols. Ambassador White and Mr. Dion occasionally observed the activity from an obscure, corner bedroom window on the second floor. Otherwise, they remained in a back room of the house where it was safer.

As the day wore, the crowd grew larger and more raucous. Many of them started drinking. By nightfall the crowd numbered about 300. It had become quite apparent that the protesters were not about to leave. Next, they began piling up combustible materials in the center of the street--wooden pallets and large pieces of scrap wood and brush. They set wooden barrels in the street to prevent traffic from passing by. They had, in fact, blocked both ends of the portion of the road that was in the front of the residence. Meanwhile, there were no police officers or military soldiers in sight.

None of us rested very well that evening. There was only a total of fifteen of us inside the compound: five Marines, including Gunny Saebo, RSO Walander, and five agents, including myself, Ambassador White, DCM Dion, and two-house staff. The Marines and DS detail kept a sharp vigil. To add to our worries, we also speculated that an attack might come from a Leftist terrorist group, while our attention was diverted to the ongoing Rightist demonstration. The demonstrators were becoming intoxicated and belligerent. They set the woodpile on fire, and in minutes a huge blaze roared in front of the residence gate. Flames leapt twenty-feet high, towering above the wall. Cinders rocketed into the night sky. The demonstrators played recorded music over the speakers and danced in the streets. Occasionally, a few fired their weapons into the air. It was unnerving. Still, we had little choice but to wait it out. By 2:00 a.m., the crowd had diminished to about 100 demonstrators. As of yet, there was no sign of Salvadoran military or police. This was worrisome to the ambassador, who was concerned that the Junta and Minister of Defense were afraid to give an order for troops to come to our aid. More and more, it looked as if we were on our own.

"Hey, Tony . . ." I quipped to RSO Walander, ". . . looks like another situation where we're defending the Alamo."

"Yah, Bowie and Crockett," he replied. We took turns getting a little rest.

Around 7:00 a.m. on Sunday morning, the gardener who also had been trapped inside the compound woke up very sick. He owned a small car, which was parked on the inside driveway. He walked up to the gate, opened the parcel window, and was able to negotiate with one of the sentinels to be allowed to leave. While one Marine opened the gate, the others stood by with M16s poised and ready to repel any attempt by demonstrators to make a charge inside. I saw the gardener drive out and onto the road. The crowd, still small and tired from being up all night, immediately surrounded his car. They forced open the trunk and thoroughly inspected the back seat, thinking that the ambassador was hiding inside. Convinced that their prize was not in the car, they let the gardener leave.

By Sunday afternoon, the crowd had swelled again to about 400 persons. They consumed the street for half a block. New protest signs appeared with anti-American slogans. A man's loud voice echoed through the loudspeakers to protest White's presence in El Salvador and blasted anti-Carter and anti-White slogans. The crowd chanted "¡White no más! ¡White no más!" ("White no more! White no more!") Next a woman stepped up to the microphone stand atop the truck's flatbed. With a sweet, almost melodic voice, she attempted to lure the security personnel outside the compound, using friendly words and stating that the protesters had no argument with the Marines, only with Ambassador White. She was a regular Tokyo Rose:

"¡Vayan a sus casas, Marines!" ("Go home, Marines!") "¡Vayan a sus esposas y sus niños!" ("Go home to your wives and children!")

At 4:00 p.m. we heard the loud blare of a truck horn. It was a troop transport truck loaded with rifle-toting soldiers passing slowly by. The crowd moved aside so the truck could pass and started cheering their arrival. We anxiously watched, hoping the soldiers would disembark and disperse the mob. No dice. The troops just sat stoically as the crowd waved and cheered. The message was clear: no one was going to come to our rescue. We were being held hostage!

As night fell on the second full day of our captivity, an even bigger bonfire was burning with more combustible materials carted in and tossed into the flames. Flames shot up beyond the peak of the roof. I could feel the intense heat from the fire roaring in the street down below--about thirty yards from my window view. The demonstrators, in an obviously aggressive show to convince all of us that they meant to keep us prisoners, parked a Volkswagen minibus parallel to and in front of the gate to block any attempt of escape.

Meanwhile, food supplies were getting desperately low inside. Feeding fifteen hostages from midday Saturday through Sunday evening had taken its toll on an already scarce food supply. Saturday was normally the day that the cook went shopping for the next week's food supplies. So, by this time, bottled drinking water was nearly gone. Mercedes, the ambassador's cook, began boiling water from a tap, which would otherwise be unsanitary for drinking.

Ambassador White had remained good-natured through all of this. His schedule that weekend was not pressing, so he had been content to wait out the demonstrators. Mrs. White had left the country earlier in March, along with the other dependents. At least White could concentrate on the events at hand without concern for his wife's safety. But Monday May 12th was fast approaching, and the ambassador had important meetings to keep. Around 7:00 p.m. he summoned Walander and me to join him and Dion in the living room.

"Tony, Steve . . . this is getting serious. Mark and I were discussing tomorrow's itinerary. I have a scheduled meeting with the junta leadership at the presidential palace in the afternoon." His voice deepened, then turned harsh:

"I can't have it publicized that the US ambassador was prevented from attending such an important meeting because he was being held captive by a few Right-wing thugs! If the international press gets hold of this incident before we get out of here, they'll have a field day!"

Then he spoke softly and deliberately. "These protestors would be spotlighted around the globe. There'll be a circus of reporters and television camera crews out in front that will dwarf the number of people out there now. Worse will be the speculation as to why the Salvadoran military or police didn't come to our aid and rescue. Our diplomatic efforts will lose all credibility. We'll be finished here." His words sounded almost reflective, as if he had visualized such an undesirable ending.

Then I realized that the telephone was still operating at the Residence, thanks to a buried cable; we also had two-way radio communication with the embassy.

"Mr. Ambassador," I offered, "we could have Colonel West call the Minister of Defense and see if they'll send some troops to clear this thing out."

"No, I don't want to do that, Steve. I've already discussed it with Mark and with the Colonel. We don't want to put the leadership in the position of giving an order that might not be obeyed by the rank and file. If their loyalties are with the protesters, then they'll disobey an order from the minister or the junta leaders, and that could lead to possible anarchy . . . or a coup."

It was true. Indications of a splintered military had become more and more visible. Hardened troops and high-level commanders supported the Right. But many of the younger, less experienced soldiers, lieutenants, and captains had come from the poor who were now siding with the Left. White did not want to put the government and military leaders in the position of having to stand by while loyalties played out over the issue of rescuing a US ambassador.

"No, boys, this time we're really on our own. You guys are going to have to figure a way to get us out of here."

The ambassador had reported our situation to the State Department Command Center in Washington. He did this by dictating a telegram over the two-way radio to the embassy's communications officer who, in turn, sent the telegram.

"Washington's aware of our situation and if we can't get out, they'll try to think of something. But right now, it's up to us." "OK, Mr. Ambassador," Tony replied. "We'll get back to you in about an hour."

At 10:00 p.m. Tony, Gunny, the other agents and I gathered in an upstairs bedroom. One of the agents said, "What about calling in more of the Marines? Have them assault the protesters with tear gas from the rear, and we'll do the same from the front."

Gunny replied with a snicker, "Only if you want to start World War III. If my guys show up outside this gate, there will surely be a confrontation."

Walander added, "There are all kinds of international agreements that prevent a country's military troops from committing any such hostilities in a foreign country. This isn't like Teheran, where we had cut off all diplomatic relations and had announced Iran as our enemy."

Tony may have been mistaken about the US having declared Iran our enemy before conducting the Delta Force strike to free the hostages, but he was right about the rest of it. Marine Security

Guards are only to be engaged in defense of the embassy or the Ambassador's Residence while stationed inside either compound, properties, which are considered to be US soil. Engaging forces outside of the compound is strictly prohibited and would be looked upon as an invasion. I spoke up.

"Last night, about 100 protestors remained in the street all night long. They got very drunk and didn't sleep much. Monday is a workday for many. I'm betting that by early tomorrow morning, before sunrise, most of the crowd will have dissipated and our chance for escape will be much improved."

The others agreed, and so set about devising a plan for our escape. Outside, the demonstration continued: loud music, hostile shouts of obscenities, the chanting of anti-American slogans, and an occasional gunshot being discharged. Around 10:30 p.m. things started quieting down, as many of the demonstrators had left. Soon the numbers of demonstrators had shrunk to about 150. The bonfire was still raging in the street, however, and the minivan was still blocking the drive entrance outside of the gate. We knew full well that we'd have to crash through these obstacles if we were to succeed in our escape. We hadn't slept in thirty-six hours. By 11:00 p.m. we had completed our escape plan. Tony and I walked into the living room and presented the scenario to Ambassador White and Mark Dion.

"What have you two got for us, Steve?" White asked.

"Well, it's not too complicated, Sir," I said. "We would like for you and Mr. Dion to simply go out into the street tonight, sing and dance with the protestors and convince them you're good guys. After all, you're both great diplomats, and you should be able to persuade them to let all of us go. How does that sound?" "Like someone's been chewing on peyote," White replied. "I didn't know it was growing in my backyard."

"Yes, Sir, in every one of those cactus plants!" Had I not been so punchy from lack of sleep, I wouldn't have been so callous with the attempt at humor. But they both seemed to enjoy it. Then, we got down to business.

"Sir, we're going to use the armored Suburban and crash out of here," I said.

"At 4:00 a.m., we'll sneak out the front door. You and Mr. Dion, and Tony and I will enter the Suburban from the tailgate door. That way, there will be only one door to close. I'll get in first and make my way up to the driver's seat, and then Tony will climb in the front. Next, we want you to get in, Mr. Ambassador. Finally, Mr. Dion gets in and quietly pulls the door closed behind him. We're asking both of you to lie sideways in the back of the Suburban. You'll both be wearing bulletproof vests. Any questions thus far?" They said no, so I continued.

"Gaines and two of the agents will follow us out with the Plymouth Fury. They'll be heavily armed. Fred will drive the limo, and it will be the third vehicle to come out. We'll all be wearing gas masks because the Marines will fire tear gas grenades into the street. Then, they'll throw open the gate, and I'll ram the Suburban into the minibus to push it out of the way. We'll speed on down the road and, if the Suburban breaks down, the limo will be the back-up vehicle to get us to the embassy. Nick and the guys in the Fury will intercept anyone who might take up chasing us."

White asked, "Have you ever done anything like this before, Steve?" I detected a distinct tone of doubt in his voice.

I lowered my eyebrows, thus allowing my forehead to exhibit a slight frown, as if to appear to be seriously contemplating his question. Then, almost simultaneously I conjured up a determined look and with a half-smile said,

"Mr. Ambassador, compared with crash and bang school at the Farm this will be a walk in the park." I went on to explain some of what I had done while in training there.

"I've heard about that training camp. Well, I hope you paid attention. Our lives are in your hands!" he said, soberly. "What about the Residence? Once the gate is opened won't the protesters invade?"

"We don't think so. We think they'll be caught by surprise and overcome with tear gas. The Marines can quickly close the gate after the last vehicle clears. Gunny will remain here with his four MSGs.

"That's right," Gunny said. "As long as we're on the Residence property, we're on US soil. Any attempt by the demonstrators to come in will be repelled." Gunny's voice was stern and determined. There was no doubt that he and the MSGs were ready to defend the Ambassador's Residence.

The ambassador spoke up. "I don't want anyone to get killed, Gunny. Use the minimum force necessary to keep them out. My God, if you shoot one or more of these people you'll destroy years of diplomacy with the Rightists in this country. We won't stand a chance at gaining their support again. Just get that damned gate closed before they know what hit them," he said with crescendo. "I don't want any of the Marines to get hurt either," White added. "You've got to keep the demonstrators out without anyone getting killed!" A mental image of what might go wrong during the escape must have come upon him, and with it he became unsettled about this part of the plan.

Gunny remained calm and replied, "We'll do our best, Sir. I don't want anyone to get killed either."

"All right then," said White. "I think we'd all better get a little rest."

The ambassador and Dion retired to their respective bedrooms around midnight. In four hours, six agents and two diplomats held hostage were going to attempt to escape their captors by breaking out of the residence. Gunny and four Marines would stay behind as defenders. We took turns getting sleep, three of us at a time, in two-hour shifts. The night wore on. Through the surveillance camera we counted about thirty protesters, mostly men, many of whom appeared to be intoxicated and standing guard in the street. That they had firearms was certain. Whether they would use them was the unnerving question.

Shortly after 4:00 a.m., I climbed behind the wheel of the Chevy Suburban. Under the cover of darkness, the others climbed in behind me. Gaines, Manning, and the other agents all got in the vehicles and quietly pulled the doors closed. The Suburban was parked about thirty feet from the gate. All of us had donned gas masks. At the same time, the Marines snuck down to the steel plated gate and quietly unlatched the twelve-inch-long bolt. In unison, drivers started their engines. Hours earlier we had turned the Suburban in the direction of the gate, ready for exit. We had also pre-positioned the two other vehicles so they were properly lined up for the escape. We had done this when the crowd was larger and still noisy.

But now, despite our stealth, the captors heard the sound of the car engines. They began counter movements. Several of the demonstrators who had been sitting or lying on the ground, jumped up, grabbing their rifles. Others started talking, hastily shouting orders. Only seconds had passed from the time we aroused them to when the moment came to roll back the gate. Several of the protestors' sentinels surged toward the opening. In response, Marines discharged three canisters of tear gas into the street. At that same precise moment, I headed the Suburban toward the minibus, slowly at first to get a proper alignment, then accelerating the car at full throttle. The glare of the headlights caught a demonstrator as he was running toward the gate. BANG! The Suburban crashed into the minibus, spinning it out of the path, and nearly catching the now retreating sentinel. The truck continued moving forward. At the moment of impact, we felt a jolt. But the armor plating and reinforced steel bumper of this three-quarter-ton truck far outmatched the minibus, easily overpowering it. Our captors became engulfed by gas and began coughing and choking, quickly becoming disoriented. I cranked the steering wheel fully to the left. Half of the Suburban rolled through the flames of the raging bonfire. Now, I was driving with half the vehicle in the road and the other half up over the curb riding on the grass. I continued accelerating to get us out of there. Tony had the barrel of the Uzi sticking out of the gun portal, ready to fire. Ambassador White and Mark Dion were hunkered down in the back. We felt another jolt, this time the vehicle rolling over some large boards, but we continued moving headlong. Next came the wooden barrels and barricades. We crashed through them. Boards and barrels flew up and rolled in every direction. I didn't want to slow down for a second because I knew Gaines and Manning were right behind me, maneuvering through the same obstacles and debris. We continued speeding away. About a quarter mile down the road, Agents Gaines and Manning radioed that they had cleared the gate and that they were right behind us. Then one of the Marines radioed that they had secured the gate and were safely inside the residence compound. No shots had been fired. From inside the Suburban, we all removed our gas masks and let loose with shouts of exaltation. We sped away toward the Chancery and to freedom. White and Dion popped their heads up and joined in the cheers of "Hooray!" We had completely surprised the captors and had made our escape!

But our cheers were short-lived. We had traveled less than two miles and were still five miles from the embassy when one of the tires on the Suburban went flat. Apparently, I had run over some nails and debris, causing the tire to puncture. The tires were the only unprotected part of the Suburban. We slowed to a crawl. The three good tires couldn't support the weight of the heavily armored vehicle. They too quickly deflated. I managed to pull the Suburban over to a curb where I told everyone to get out. Just then, Manning pulled up with the black, armored Cadillac.

"You boys need a ride?" he asked with a grin.

"Just get us to the embassy," I answered. Relieved, I felt the adrenalin quickly dissipating. Tony and I squeezed into the front seat of the limo. White and Dion got into the back seat. The other agents got into the Plymouth Fury when it pulled up. Off we went, speeding to safety. After eight miles of driving, we finally arrived intact. The time was 5:10 a.m. Heavily armed Marines greeted us. Our two-vehicle motorcade then descended into the underground garage. After exiting the vehicles, Ambassador White and Mark Dion lingered for a minute beside the limo. White spoke: "Well, Mark, this is where we were three days ago, when we were advised to leave early to avoid a demonstration. Three days later we're back at the same place after being held hostage. We never should have left!" White bellowed out the words in an all too apparent release of all the built-up adrenalin. It's a crazy business we're in, don't you think?"

"When I signed on to join the Foreign Service, I didn't expect anything like this," Dion remarked. "Shouldn't we be eligible for some kind of special compensation or award?" he joshed. "How about hazardous, duty-pay?"

"They won't even want to know about this back in D.C.," White said. "Nothing has been accomplished to better our relations with El Salvador today."

Later that morning I requested the local Salvadoran head of the motor pool at the embassy to take another man with him, and go out and change the tire on the Suburban, then return it to the embassy. I wondered if it had been found by any of the protestors and perhaps burned. Later that day it was sitting in the embassy garage, freshly washed and waxed. The next day, Tuesday, May 13, 1980, a headline in the *Miami Herald* read, "US Envoy Rescued from Rightist Siege at Salvadoran Home." The article began with the words, "US Marines and Ambassador Robert E. White's bodyguards used tear gas and a bullet-proof truck Monday to break a siege of Rightists, diplomatic sources said." We didn't return the ambassador to his Residence for several days, and later that night we drove him to a safe house. On the way there White and I talked about the headline.

"Did you see the headline in the *Miami Herald*, Steve?"

"Yes I did, Mr. Ambassador. What did you think of it?"   "I liked it!" he proclaimed cheerfully. "It sure read more favorably than how it could have had things not turned out so well."   He was so right. Many headlines to come out of El Salvador during that period had reported far more gruesome results--kidnappings, bombings, and murders.

Robert E. White served as US ambassador to El Salvador until June 1981. After President Reagan took office in January 1981, he directed his Secretary of State, General Alexander Haig, to review all the ambassadorial appointments made by Reagan's predecessor, Jimmy Carter. Reagan disagreed with Carter's softer, less direct, foreign relations approach, preferring ambassadors who were in line with his straightforward foreign policy initiatives. General Haig yanked several ambassadors and replaced them with Reagan appointees. Ambassador White was one such casualty. Fortunately for White, he was a political casualty—not a casualty of kidnapping or assassination. Lord knows that terrorist elements from both the Right and the Left had devised many plans to kill him while I was protecting him. They never succeeded.

CHAPTER 22

PEACE CORPS IN PERIL

No day was routine. With spouses and children gone, the remaining embassy diplomatic corps worked even longer hours. Tony and I were nearly always engaged in matters of protecting the diplomats or the embassy. The violence around us grew steadily worse, each act of savagery turning more and more gruesome by the day. Continued and escalating threats against US corporations with employees in El Salvador led many companies to cease operations and pull out. Leftist guerrillas manipulated by Communist handlers demanded the departure of "Yankee

Imperialism." My job, in part, was to provide security updates to the American businessmen in El Salvador. As violence increased, Tony and I received many visits from corporate security managers eager for detailed information as to our up-to-date assessments and advisories of the security situation. As US companies pulled out, targets for kidnappings and bombings became scarce. The US embassy stood virtually alone as the symbol (and therefore the target) of US presence, along with the one ill-fated McDonald's restaurant in San Salvador. Apparently the "Golden Arches" emblem was enough of a symbol of American capitalism to incite the terrorists. It was firebombed four times. Ironically, a

Salvadoran businessman owned the restaurant. He finally gave up keeping the restaurant open after the fourth firebombing.

The Chancery was the target of Leftist extremists numerous times and was attacked four times in 1980. One attack occurred one day in May 1980 when a group of guerrillas in a speeding pickup truck attacked the US embassy. One gunman sprayed the embassy with machine gun fire while two others tossed bombs from the back of the pickup. The bombs exploded on the outside of the reinforced concrete embassy walls, thus causing little damage and no injuries. Still, the sounds of the explosions, which I witnessed from my office that day, called for full defensive positioning by embassy personnel and Marine guards. Marines were stationed on the rooftop to lob tear gas canisters, if necessary. Other embassy personnel formed fire brigades in pre-designated locations. Fortunately, there were no more attacks that day. Another attack occurred on September 16, 1980. Leftist guerrillas, firing Chinese-made anti-tank rockets, blasted a nine-foot-wide hole in the embassy wall. The first rocket destroyed an empty office on the third floor. The empty office was located within only a few feet of the Ambassador's Office and occupied at the time by his secretary. Though the rocket penetrated the outer wall, causing a gaping hole, it failed to explode. A second rocket fell on the roof but did not explode. Again, through good fortune, no one was killed or injured. Later, witnesses reported that they saw four young men in a blue pickup truck launch the rockets from about one hundred yards out.

The US ambassador and embassy diplomats and staff weren't the only targets of attack. In a twelve-month period from December 1979 to December 1980, hundreds of innocent Salvadoran citizens were murdered. The embassies of Panama, South Africa, and Spain were taken siege at different times with their ambassadors taken hostage. Riots also took the lives of many innocent people. Troops were being ambushed in rural areas as rebels raided their outposts. Each day the newspapers carried stories of more slayings by both Rightist and Leftist death squads. Salvadoran government officials were gunned down in their homes or on the streets, as were Leftist political and guerrilla leaders. Decapitated and carved bodies were found floating in drainage ditches, or dumped in street gutters, or hanging from overpasses. Leftist guerrillas seized radio stations for hours so they could broadcast their messages of rebellion to the populace.

A full-scale civil war was fast emerging. An Associated Press headline read, "Violence Is Tearing El Salvador Apart." The numbers of dead in weekly bloody gun skirmishes rose from a few to scores.

I vividly recall coming upon a gruesome scene one morning in June of 1980. I was driving from my house to the Ambassador's Residence. As I approached a railroad viaduct overpass that stretched above the road, I saw something hanging from it. As I got closer, I could see that it was the bloody, headless corpse of a male adult. The rope by which it was hanging had been tied under his arms. The corpse, covered in blood-soaked clothing, was dangling above my car as I high-tailed it with the utmost haste underneath the horrifying sight and on through the viaduct.   Tony and I had our hands full: we were in charge of managing the protection of the remaining diplomats, the embassy, the Ambassador's Residence, and other US government employees and buildings in El Salvador.

The Peace Corps Volunteer (PCV) building was one of those other US government office facilities for which we were responsible for safeguarding. It was located a block away from the Chancery. One day I received an emergency call from a worker there. The caller frantically alerted me to an explosion that had occurred moments earlier inside the building. She said that some volunteers were possibly trapped inside on the second floor and that a fire had broken out. As I dashed out of the office, I relayed a message to Tony and told him to meet me there. I ran out of the Chancery and down the block to the smoking building. Peace Corps Director Sylvia Perez was standing on the sidewalk in front of the building with a contingent of several volunteers.

"Is everyone out?" I asked.

"No," she exclaimed. "Two volunteers are still in there."
I ran into the building. The first floor was not burning. I ran up a staircase to the second floor and found a couple of volunteers, both women in their early twenties, wrestling with a fire extinguisher, trying to extinguish the fire. I rushed up to them and said, "Leave, now! Don't worry about the fire!"

I grabbed one of them by the hand and led her down the staircase and outside. "Is anyone else in there? I asked.

"No one," the young volunteers replied.

Fire trucks rolled up to the burning building and firemen charged inside. An hour later the blaze was safely extinguished. Tony and I had been standing outside with the Peace Corps staff when the Fire Chief walked up to us. He was carrying a liquor bottle, stuffed with a gasoline-soaked cloth. He handed it to Tony.

"This one failed to explode," he said in Spanish.

Tony and I walked into the building and up the stairs to the room that had been torched with the Molotov cocktails. An open window in the room, which faced an alley below, told the story. From that day forth we placed Salvadoran police guards around the building that housed the Peace Corps.

It was a rain-drenched day in June of 1980 when the Assistant Director of the Peace Corps, Jan Allister, walked into the RSO's office. She expressed grave concern that a female American volunteer had not called in for several days. Peace Corps volunteers were instructed to call into the headquarters from their posts out in the countryside several times during the week. The Peace Corps was in the process of downsizing and, for fear of their safety, had pulled many volunteers out of the countryside and into San Salvador. As violence grew, the Peace Corps began sending them back home to the US. Others, still in the outlying villages, had been given two-way radios in case phone lines went down.

But this volunteer was unaccounted for too long, and Ms. Allister was worried. Tony asked me to help her.

"We haven't heard from her by phone or by radio," Jan informed me. "It's been nearly a week. I feel I must go back up there."

"Where is she?" I asked.

"In San Marcos," Jan replied. Jan showed me the location of the village on a map hanging on a wall in my office. Agent Manning, who closely read all daily Intelligence reports, had been applying colored pins to the map: yellow for terrorist-controlled strongholds, green for gun skirmishes between rebels and military or police patrols, and red for extreme violence and murder of innocents by rebels. Red and yellow pins were stabbed into the mapped area in and around San Marcos, as was the road that one must take to reach the village.

"There's been a lot of fighting going on up there," I said to Jan. "Has the volunteer reported any fighting or rebel activity during the past phone calls?"

"They're instructed not to say anything about political unrest or military activity," she replied. "We don't want a conversation to be overheard and have someone thinking our volunteer is a spy for the US government."

"No, certainly not. What do you want to do?"

"Well, it's been raining heavily. I'm not even sure I can make it up those muddy clay and dirt roads. From past journeys I know there's at least one bridge. When the rains are heavy, the creek will rise over the bridge and flood the banks, probably making the bridge impassable. I'll take a jeep and a radio. If I can't get to the village, maybe I can get close enough to at least reach her by radio. When the weather dries out, I'll run up there again and check on her."

Jan Allister was one tough lady. Petite in size, she stood only 5'2" and weighed barely over 100 lb. Her dark black hair was cut very short. She was about thirty and had an olive complexion, which made me think she may have been of Mediterranean descent. The Salvadoran sun had made her skin color even darker. Her near-perfect, fluent Spanish convinced me that she could have passed for an indigenous Salvadoran, which could help her if she got into a tight spot. I, on the other hand, was a typical "Yankee Imperialist" looking kind of guy, with my Anglo-European complexion, blond hair and blue eyes. Being average in height—5'10"and weighing 185 lb.—and working for the US embassy, I'd be the obvious choice for hostage taking. Jan was dedicated to a life of leading Peace Corps volunteers in Central America. She had been in the Peace Corps for ten years, and I respected her dedication and knowledge greatly. Now, this peaceful warrior was about to go out into the war-ravaged countryside on a mission to rescue a volunteer. I couldn't let her do it alone.

I had to go with her.

"Jan, I don't think you should go up there by yourself. I would appreciate it if you'd wait until later today when I can go with you.

I'll escort the ambassador home and then meet you somewhere . . . say around 6:00?"

"Steve, I'm not asking you to go. I just wanted you to know what I was going to be doing so that you guys will know where I'm going."

Her excuse wasn't convincing enough. Of course, she hoped one of us would go with her. Why else would she have stopped by the office when there were others at the PCV Center to whom she could have relayed her plans? But she was very independent and didn't want to appear in need of anyone else's assistance in the matter, which she considered her personal responsibility.

"Jan, it's no trouble. I'm always concerned for the safety of the volunteers. Tell me where to meet you, and I'll bring along an extra radio and a little fire power." I knew Jan wasn't fond of guns, but I didn't think she'd mind if it might make the difference between living and dying. We agreed to meet in the hotel parking lot at the Camino Real in downtown San Salvador.

Promptly at 6 p.m. we met. I locked my car and hopped in the passenger front seat of the jeep. The overcast sky looked threatening, and Jan had secured the canvas top so we'd keep dry. I laid the Uzi on the floor between my feet.

"All ready!" I said cheerfully. Normally, the drive would have taken about an hour, but the roads were rarely maintained, and most of the roadways which were dirt turned into mud when it rained, and the rain had begun pouring down. It never let up. By the time we reached the less traveled, mountainous dirt and clay roads it was dark. Rain was beating down on the jeep's canvas top and driving these now slippery roads became treacherous. Regardless, Jan and the jeep were handling the muddy, slimy road surface quite well. As we twisted and turned our way over the rocky, rough roads we made light talk and got to know one another better.

"This hard rain will keep the army in their barracks and rebels in their houses tonight," I chuckled.

"Then I'm glad it's raining," Jan said.

By 8:00 p.m., after traveling sixty miles in two hours, we came to the creek that Jan had talked about. "The village is just a few miles beyond that bridge--if we can only get across. I'll see if I can reach Stacey on the radio."

We stopped at the bridge, a thirty-foot long, six-foot wide rickety, wooden structure, with torrents of water flowing swiftly over it. Jan tried several times to call the volunteer, but there was no response. My stomach felt queasy, like one might feel before performing in front of an audience. But this nervousness was due to thinking there might be something seriously wrong in that village. We knew that soldiers were pilfering some villages, raping the women and killing the men if they thought them to be aiding rebels. I worried that this fate may have befallen Stacey and her village compatriots. I was more determined than ever to reach our destination.

"The creek's rising," Jan said, "and, if we are able to cross it by the time we check on Stacey and come back, we may not be able to get through it again."

"Let's not delay then," I said. "I have to be back tomorrow for the morning escort."

Jan made sure the four-wheel drive was in its lowest gear ratio and began creeping across the bridge. Water gushed beneath the tires. The creek appeared to be surging as we crossed, but we made it to the other side. We continued driving the jeep upward on the winding, dark road. Even with headlights we could barely see ahead through the downpour of rain. We went another mile and rounded a bend in the road, only to encounter a roadblock. But it wasn't like the ones I had encountered in training at the Farm. This one was a fallen tree, about ten inches in diameter and twelve feet long.

I got out and tossed a rain parka hood over my head. I grabbed the cable on the winch, which was mounted on the front bumper of the jeep, unraveled it and hooked it around one end of the tree. Jan expertly drove the jeep in reverse and brought the tree to one side of the road, with enough clearance so we could pass. The towering and eerie silhouettes of mammoth boulders and rock-solid hills engulfed us. The road, too, was so narrow it seemed barely passable.

As I stood outside, a feeling came over me as if I was being watched all the while.

"Great job," I said as I hastened into the jeep.

"Same for you," she replied. "Now, let's get out of here."

We forged on without encountering any other obstacles. Some thirty minutes later, we arrived in the little village of San Marcos. The village was nothing more than a hodgepodge collection of clay adobe buildings with thatched roofs. These cabañas extended on either side of the dirt road, stretching for hundreds of feet. The buildings were nearly pitch dark save for a few candles and oil lamps burning inside. All power was out due to the storm. As we rolled slowly down the street it made me think of a scene from an old Western movie. The street looked like one that might be depicted as dimly lit and deserted, save for the two gunfighters. Jan kept going.

"She lives with a family at the edge of town. We'll have to go to the end of this road and turn up a two track, which will take us another five hundred feet uphill."

Jan found the two-track road. She geared down and climbed the jeep ever upward. We stopped outside the house. The door swung open and there stood Stacey, ever surprised by Jan's sudden presence. They exchanged warm hugs and greetings. We learned that her radio battery had gone dead and the phone service for the few phones that were in the town had been wiped out by the storm.   Nonetheless, she was fine. No rebels or soldiers had been through. Stacey was in good spirits. Jan wanted her to return with us, but the determined volunteer persuaded Jan to let her stay in the village for a few more days. She explained that her project was nearly done and that she really wanted to see it finished. Stacey, who was a graduate of Michigan State University with a degree in Engineering, had been coaching the villagers how to build a fresh water viaduct. When finished, it would transport fresh water mechanically so that the villagers would no longer have to carry water over a half of a mile.

From my point of view as a Security Officer, I would have ordered her immediately into that jeep. Things were way too dangerous for a young American woman to remain in such hostile conditions. But I came to witness over and over again, throughout my time in El Salvador, the faith and perseverance of people like Stacey, Jan Allister, the dedicated missionaries, the teachers at the American School, and so many other Americans who had come to serve in El Salvador. They believed in what they were doing. Such people earnestly wanted to make a difference to help improve the lives and fate of the people there. They did so in spite of the constant threat of danger to their own lives.

Jan sided with Stacey probably because she saw some of herself in the volunteer. We had brought two charged batteries for the radio.

"Now stay in touch with me daily," Jan commanded as the two of them embraced for the last time.

"I will call every day," said Stacey. "Thanks, Jan, for letting me stay. Thank you too, Steve, for helping Jan."

"Take care, Stacey," I said. "We'll see you in a few days back in San Salvador." Stacey was to return to San Salvador by bus after the rain stopped and the roads dried.

"The annual party for PCVs and embassy guests is next week, Saturday," Jan told Stacey. "We'll look forward to seeing you there."

With that, we bid each other goodbye and drove off. The drive back seemed ever so much simpler, even joyful. We laughed and joked at just about everything from the rising creek to my image of gunfighters in a western town. Our nerves were calming down from all the adrenalin rushing through our bodies. Jan pulled the jeep up next to my car in the dimly lit hotel parking lot. It was already after midnight. The rain had stopped and a sweet smell of freshly watered flowers and grass filled the air. She turned off the motor. We both sat for a minute in silence contemplating what we had accomplished. She put her hand on my shoulder.

"I wouldn't have made it without you, Steve." Her brown eyes shone with tears. "You're a great guy. Thank you, thank you very much."

She was filled with emotion as she leaned over and kissed me on the cheek. I reached back and gave her a hug. We held each other for a brief time.

"I'm really glad I could be of help, Jan. You're an amazing person. I really admire you and all that you do."

"Hey, Steve," she said softly as the tension released and she became relaxed, "will you please come to our annual spring party next week? I'd really like it if you would. Please ask Tony to come and the other agents, too. It will be a good time!"   "Providing I'm not needed elsewhere or on duty for the ambassador, I'd like very much to come," I replied. "Speaking of the ambassador, he'll be looking to see me on his front doorstep in a few hours. I'd better be getting on home."

"Steve, I'm not going to go to my house tonight. I think I'll just go inside the hotel and check into a room. I'm too tired to do anything more. How far do you live from here?"   "About three miles," I said.

"What about the curfew?" she asked?

I had forgotten that San Salvador was under a strict government curfew forbidding any street traffic after midnight. To drive home could mean a run in with trigger-happy police or soldiers. After the attack on the motorcade, I didn't need another experience like that again.

"Would you like to stay with me here, tonight? My agency will pay for the room. I'll get one with two beds. It would make sense, wouldn't it?"

"I suppose it would, Jan. There's no real reason I have to go home tonight. I can return in the morning. The curfew ends at 6:00 a.m." I had been living alone at my house for several months since the time my wife and child, and the other American dependents had been evacuated from El Salvador.

We locked the jeep up and walked together into the hotel. Once in the room I went over to the mini-bar. We were hungry, but there was no food to eat other than chips, nuts, and pretzels. We laughed about the gourmet meal we were about to consume. Jan made herself a Rum and Coke while I mixed a Johnny Walker Scotch with a splash of water and ice.

"This was a good idea, Jan. Thanks for the thought." The last thing either of us wanted to do after what transpired that night was to drive through perilous dark streets to our respective empty houses.

Camaraderie with another warrior who has shared an experience, as we did that night, comes in different forms. For us it came in a feeling of deep, mutual respect and relief that all had gone well, and in the safety and comfort we felt by staying together for the rest of the night. We each finished our drinks and exchanged experiences about our lives and world travels. Suddenly, we were overcome with mutual exhaustion. I slipped off my shoes and lay down on one of the beds. Jan relaxed on the other bed. Soon we both had fallen asleep.

Early the next morning I returned home. I showered, dressed, put on my bullet-proof vest, checked my weapons, and drove over to the Ambassador's Residence. I was ready to face another day of guarding and protecting while remaining hopeful that I'd live to see another day and the eventual return to my wife and son.

EPILOGUE

One of my goals in writing this book was to provide the reader with insight into the world of dignitary protection and a sense of some of what occurs therein. When you attend a political rally for a world leader or see such an event on television, you will be ever wiser as to what each of the men and women who are charged with the protection of these leaders have accomplished in training and experience. I hope that you have come to appreciate the dedication and bravery demonstrated by DS Special Agents, the diplomats of the US Foreign Service, and Marine Security Guards who serve all over the world. Let us not forget to recognize the Foreign Service spouses and children who are in harm's way and who are called on to make sacrifices in being separated from their loved ones.

Finally, each of us must practice being your own bodyguard. Our surroundings are becoming increasingly unsafe. Be aware of who is around you and what they are doing. Avoid becoming a creature of habit. One in ten persons in the United Sates has been the victim of a rape, robbery, burglary, or assault. The certainty of the future is that terrorism within and outside of the US will harm and kill more Americans. Don't become the next statistic.

SOURCES

Buena Vista Pictures, *The Recruit*. Hollywood: 2003. Bureau of Diplomatic Security. *Lethal Terrorist Actions against Americans:1973-1985*. Washington, D.C., US Department of State, Threat Analysis Division, Diplomatic Security Service.

Congressional Quarterly. "The Middle East: Seventh Edition." Washington, D.C. 1991.

Dean, John. *writ.news.findlaw.com/dean/20061006. html.*

Devine, Frank. *El Salvador: Embassy under Attack.* New York: Vantage Press, 1981.

Fetherling, George. *The Book of Assassins: A Biographical Dictionary from Ancient Times to the Present.* New York:
   John Wiley & Sons, 2001.

Gibbs, Nancy, and Michael Duffy. "The Other Born Again President." *Time Magazine*, January 04, 2007.

Isaacson, Walter. *Kissinger: A Biography.* New York:
   Simon & Schuster, 1992.

Paramount Pictures. *Clear and Present Danger.*
   Hollywood: 1994.

Scahill, Jeremy. *Blackwater: The Rise of the World's Most
   Powerful Mercenary Army.* New York: Nation Books, 2007.

Warner Brothers, *Proof of Life.* Hollywood: 2000.

Warner Brothers, *Argo*, Hollywood: 2012.

GLOSSARY

AIC.   Agent in Charge

ARSO. Assistant Regional Security Officer

BPR.   Popular Revolutionary Bloc

CFO.   Chicago Field Office

DSS.   Diplomatic Security Service

DS.   Diplomatic Security

EOD.   Explosive Ordnance Device

FARN. Armed Forces of National Resistance

FPL.   Popular Liberation Forces ("Farabundo Martí")

MSG.   Marine Security Guard PCV Peace Corps Volunteer

RSO.   Regional Security Officer

SA.   Special Agent

SAIC.   Special Agent in Charge

SST   Security Support Team (a US military unit)

TS.   TOP SECRET

ABOUT THE AUTHOR

Steven M. Schenck was born, raised, and educated in Western Michigan. He graduated from Grand Valley State University. He served as a police officer and as a deputy sheriff, before a providential encounter with a "congressman" later to become President Gerald R. Ford, lead to an appointment as Special Agent. During his tenure with Diplomatic Security, he was a Senior Resident Agent of the Detroit office and an Agent in Charge of numerous protective security details. From 1978 to 1981 the author served as Chief of the Ambassador's Security and as a Regional Security Officer in El Salvador, during a raging civil war.

His list of Protectees includes three Secretaries of State, the family of the Shah of Iran, First Lady Imelda Marcos of the Philippines, Prince Rainier and Princess Grace of Monaco, Prince Charles (formerly the Prince of Wales, currently the King of England), Shimon Peres, Foreign Minister and (in 2007) President of Israel, Foreign Ministers of Japan, Syria, Argentina, Venezuela, the King and Queen of Spain, the family of President Anwar Sadat of Egypt, and others. The author has escorted foreign dignitaries on visits to the White House and into the Oval Office during state meetings with three sitting presidents: Nixon, Ford, and Carter. His work has taken him to over forty countries. More recently, he has been an international security consultant for Fortune 100 companies and a private security contractor for the US Government. Mr. Schenck lives and writes in northern Michigan, (beautiful, Benzie County), and in Grand Rapids, MI.